FOLLOWING THE BELLS

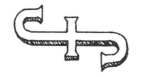

Johnny Jones'
Double Lazy J Brand

Johnny Alberta Jones
(1918-1993)

FOLLOWING THE BELLS

Traveling High Sierra Wilderness Trails

By Johnny Jones

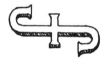

As told to Dwight H. Barnes

Library of Congress Catalog Card Number 94-70145
ISBN 0-9640058-0-8

Published by

Dwight H. Barnes
42784 Knoll Road
Oakhurst, CA 93644-9611

Manufactured in the United States of America
by Ponderosa Printing
40531 Hwy. 41 Suite B • P. O. Box 670
Oakhurst, California 93644

INTRODUCTION

Mules and horses were a part of Johnny Jones' life since early childhood. Long before he entered high school, he started following the long ears riding a mower and rake cutting alfalfa on the family farm.

In the 60-plus years that followed, Jones, who sometimes was called "Jackass Johnny" in school, became widely known as one of the leading High Sierra guides and packers, a respected mule judge and breeder of world champion performance and racing mules.

Johnny died July 25, 1993 as the writing phase of this book was getting well under way. Based on a series of tape-recorded interviews conducted over a span of nearly three years, this is his story about his beloved Sierra and the years when the bells of a mule train or grazing livestock were his favorite music.

I wish to express my deep appreciation to his family for its support and encouragement and the use of family photographs. Most helpful were several of Johnny's friends, especially Wayne Tex of Bishop. Wayne was 12 years old in 1953, when Johnny first established his own independent pack station at Mugler Meadow. Wayne started working for Johnny that year and stayed until Johnny sold out. Wayne provided important photos and accounts of experiences he shared with Johnny. Bob Barrett of Hornitos, Yosemite packer, poet, teacher and author, also helped to keep me straight on horsemanship and the back country. Western Outdoor Artist Keith Soward was most generous, drawing the cover art and the winter roundup. Cat Denning of Coarsegold also offered artwork and Mike Jones of Ponderosa Printing provided layout advice and desktop publishing services.

Yosemite Park Historian Jim Snyder, a veteran trail builder, gave welcome historical and editorial advice. Two good friends, Earlene Ward, editor of the Sierra Star, and Mary Snyder of Bass Lake performed valuable service in proof reading the manuscript, and the Coarsegold Historical Society provided photos and information from its interviews with Johnny.

I am indebted to all of you.

Dwight H. Barnes
January, 1994

Loretta

FORWARD

Whenever mountain people, ranchers and packers gather around a campfire, the name Johnny Jones inevitability comes up.

A small boy with an asthmatic condition came to the Sierra with an old family friend, Obert Bundy. Then, going on to live with Tom and Ella Jones of Beasore Meadows, Johnny began his long tenure in the Sierra.

Old timers used to say that this small frail boy didn't cast much of a shadow, but before it was over Johnny cast a very big shadow over the mountains he loved. He was a mountain legend – packer, mule and mountain man, a people person.

Through the years, Johnny packed for a lot of well-known people. Ronald Reagan, Fibber McGee and Molly, Stewart Hamlin who wrote the famous song "This Old House" were just a few of the many that Johnny came in contact with, making friendships that lasted a life time. Johnny was strict about taking care of the people when he was out in the mountains. "Take care of the people first," he would always say.

All through the Sierra, Johnny had trails where trails didn't exist, places you would think it impossible for stock to travel, and when he went through he left no trace that he had ever been there. "Bushwacking" Johnny would call it. Many a time, Johnny was called out to track a lost or injured person, using skills he learned from the Indian people he was raised with. Johnny always was quick to give credit to these people for teaching him the ways of the mountains.

Owner and operator of a pack station, he also bred and raised mules. Johnny was an extraordinary mule man with a good eye for quality. When he couldn't supply enough from his own herd, he went to Arkansas, bought and traded for them. That really must have been something, Johnny dealing with the slick mule men of Arkansas. I doubt if any of those boys got up early enough to beat Johnny in a deal.

A judge for many years at the famed Bishop Mule Days, he was with it from the start. He also was a founding member of the American Mule Association. His eye for a good mule set the standard of excellence for mule judging as it is today. The success of these two organizations had a lot to do with Johnny's contributions.

Johnny always was concerned about the well-being of the mountains, so that future generations could enjoy them. Leave no trace, he always would say. He was the type of person who, if while riding along a trail he saw a candy or gum wrapper, or cigarette butt, he would get off and put it in his pocket.

Often, he was referred to by people who knew him as an environmentalist.

If he was, he had common sense to go with it.

Dwight Barnes, no stranger to mountains himself, has done a superb job in getting Johnny's story in book form. So enjoy. It's one of a kind and the end of an era.

Bob Barrett
Hornitos, California

A recent photo with one of the last Jones-bred mules. *(Photo by Gene Rose)*

TABLE OF CONTENTS

*Cover drawing: Johnny Jones and the world champion
performance mule, Rabbit, by Keith Soward of Oakland.*

At tree line.

'Where God Lives'

Yosemite National Park Historian Jim Snyder recalls meeting on the trail a lone back packer who asked, "Where can I camp?"

"Anywhere," was the answer. "You can camp anywhere."

"Well I kind of like a fire ring. It's reassuring."

Snyder, who had spent 27 seasons in the high country repairing Yosemite trails, soon realized the hiker was looking for Bridalveil campground, queried, "Why do you want to go there?"

"Well, I think they got showers, an outhouse and all that stuff," was the hiker's explanation who added, "Where can I go where there aren't any mosquitoes?"

"Home!" was Snyder's disgusted response. "I didn't know what else to tell him," he told me later. "You know, you sleep high where it's cool and they'll be gone by night. In the daytime, just put on some mosquito goop and enjoy the country. He couldn't deal with that."

In many ways this is the story of the High Sierra today. With more than 70,000 people entering Yosemite's wilderness for overnight stays each year, too many come to the mountains to "experience" Nature and yet demand all the comforts of home.

Although I was introduced to the wilderness at a time when there were not as many people, it is not the numbers that worry me today, but the way in which people treat the wilderness. They don't learn the laws of the land, how to live in and protect the environment. Too often they congregate in large groups. Something called "fast-packing" is being promoted, backpackers jogging wilderness trails to get over them as fast as they can.

The value of wilderness is not trying to see how much ground you can cover, how fast you can climb a cliff or a peak, but in taking the time to gather in the strength with which the mountains can renew you so you may face life in today's high pressure society.

People go to the ocean or the mountains for vacations. The sea is wonderful, but it is restless, constantly moving. It is only in the mountains that one can find true peace. I know we can't stop people from coming to the mountains and we shouldn't because that's the only place in God's world where people are all equal, where they can keep their sanity. In spite of the numbers, which are sure to grow, quiet places for renewal away from crowds still can be found, but we do have to have rules to protect them.

I was fortunate to have known the High Sierra 60 or more years ago when there was a true wilderness, maybe not designated by law, but created by nature, and I was able to grow up in that environment.

My introduction to the mountains came when I was only eight or 10 years old. Growing up on a farm near Patterson, I developed a serious allergy to alfalfa. A neighbor who had retired from farming and moved to Coarsegold, Obert Bundy, first took me to Beasore Meadows, which then was pretty much the end of the road east of Bass Lake.

When I saw those meadows and tall trees, it was just like heaven: Clear sky, clean, cool air. Determined to stay there where I believed God lived, I tried to make myself useful around the Beasore store owned by Tom and Ella Jones.

E. T. Whitfield, an old cattleman, told me years later:

"You were so small you didn't even make a shadow. But, you were out there picking up even those little bitty bits of papers and just raking around. I noticed how you always left the pine needles, but took away anything that did not belong there. You were just like a finicky old lady."

I've always been that way. I was weird, I guess, but I always wanted the mountains to be the way they were before anyone got here. I didn't want pine needles raked away from a tree. If someone brushed needles and branches aside

Beasore Meadows, "Where God lives."

2

for a bedroll, I wanted them put back when he moved on. I thought God put those needles where they had fallen and if He dropped them that way, they belonged there.

As I got older, branching out into the forests, I just got more fussy. Maybe, I was an environmentalist before my time, but when I see the beautiful lakes, the forests, I just call it God's country. But, I also know that we must take care of it and if telling my story helps in some small way to accomplish this, then I will be happy.

It was a rough old road getting into Beasore, but many San Joaquin Valley families had been coming to camp for the season every summer for several years. As a result, I grew up with kids from the Green, Ceroni, Oberti and other families from Madera and Fresno. Later, when I started as a guide, I packed for them, for their children and sometimes even for their grandchildren. Thinking of that makes me feel like an old buzzard.

As a kid, I just rousted around and did most anything to help out. Thirty or 40 years ago, I was told that I was supposed to be the kid in a book for teenagers "You Just Never Know," written by Marian Garthwaite. She was the Madera County children's librarian and lived around here and wrote about Coarsegold and other areas, including Beasore where she often camped. I don't know, but like "Zeke" in the book I always was picking up things and doing whatever needed to be done.

Tom and Ella Jones kept two or three old cows, half Hereford and kind of wild, for milking. Ella was not well and one day Tom asked me, "Can you milk like I milk?"

That was no problem. At home, even when I was a little kid, milking was a matter of survival. He tested me out and, oh man, I could spray out there, so I got that job. I milked the cows, strained and bottled milk for the store. The camper kids would help me. In the evening, we would round up the calves and put them in a corral away from their mamas so there would be plenty of milk in the morning.

Of course, it got more interesting when the Jones' own cows got a little dry and we went out and rounded up a range cow with a calf. We'd tie her horns to a fence, tie up one leg and away we would go, us kids taking turns milking on one side with a calf bumping on the other. It was quite a race.

Today, the kids would say that the Sierra gave me a "high," and I guess that's true because I was so high and happy in the mountains, they are so beautiful, as I keep saying, just like heaven.

I learned so much from the people who came there. Cattlemen stopped by when moving their herds to summer ranges. Old sheepherders came back for a last look at the mountains. Campers stayed at Beasore year after year. They all would sit around the campfire outside the store and talk. I'd just listen, listen, listen. Even when I was a little kid, they intrigued me. I loved to hear their stories. Sure, the old timers told some fairy tales, but when I was a little kid some times I wasn't sure just which were true.

Like the time an old, old prospector, John Beck – oh, he was some story teller – told me about hitting some rich, rich ore up at Iron Mountain above 77 Corral. When he prospected, he always hiked, carrying a rifle in his arm and leading a donkey.

I was just beginning to take trips on my own when he said to me: "Son, when you're up that way I want you to do something for me. Years ago, I was coming across a stretch where the iron ore was thick. My old burro just stopped, wouldn't move. I couldn't see any reason for it, but he wouldn't go. I pulled on the lead rope and pulled and pulled, but he just stood there.

"Finally, I put down my rifle and pulled real hard with both arms and that donk moved all right. I just pulled him out of his shoes. The four shoes were still there on the ground where he had been standing. Then, when I reached down to pick up my rifle, I couldn't budge it.

"That iron ore was so heavy that it acted like a magnet. I imagine those shoes and rifle are still where they were. Now when you are up there, I want you to look around and find them."

Other times, were different. There was talk about how to handle stock and where the best fishing was and trails which were good and bad and early days in the mountains. I listened because those old timers knew so much and I had to learn if I was going to grow up to be a guide. I wish now that I listened more carefully to the stories about the old times because history is so important.

I do remember when the family of an old, old Basque sheep-herder, Mike Etcheverria, brought him to Beasore to see again the country in which he had herded sheep for Miller and Lux.

He told about driving a band of 2,000 sheep from Tres Pinos on the West Side of the San Joaquin Valley through Fresno. He said they held the band and grazed on a field where the Fresno County Courthouse now stands. They moved across into the hills, up the San Joaquin River to 77 Corral and then across the Sierra high country. They went as far as the West Walker River and then back through Sonora Pass and across the Valley. I didn't know where the Walker River was then, so I didn't realize until years later what a trip that was.

And, of course, there were many Indians who worked for Jones and others in the meadows. The Indians were the greatest, finest mountain people ever.

4

Because I was the unofficial foster son of Tom Jones, the Indians accepted me. To this day, many people believe that I am Indian. When people ask me, I say, "No, but I wish I were." But in truth I am Portuguese, my true family name is Alberta.

Old John Beasore was one of the first white men to settle in what now is Eastern Madera County. He was involved in many things, including building the first schoolhouse in 1868. In the 1860s he began to run cattle in Beasore Meadows, which he eventually owned. He was French, married to an Indian.

Tom Jones, Sr. came here from Wales. According to what I have been told, he was the first white man in Madera County to marry an Indian princess.

Although young Tom Beasore was a little older than my foster father, John Beasore hired him summers for a dollar a month plus board to help out and to be company for his son. That way, the two boys pretty much grew up living and working together at Beasore Meadows in the summer and as neighbors on ranches in the Coarsegold–Hawkins Valley area in the winter. They were like brothers and when Tom Beasore, Jr. died, Tom Jones, Jr. inherited Beasore Meadows.

Jones and his first wife, Ella, operated the store, pack station, some cabins and a camping area at Beasore during the summers. While still in grammar school, I went home each winter to Patterson, but I returned to Beasore every summer. Gradually, I took on more jobs around Jones' Store and their campground. After my first year at Patterson High School, I stayed in the mountains with the Jones year round. That last year of school was important, however. I remember in Ag classes, all we talked about were beef and dairy cattle until one day I asked the teacher, "A lot of us kids grew up with draft animals, horses and mules. We work with them all the time at home but we never talk about them in class. How come?"

The teacher sent away to the Universities of Missouri and Kentucky for books on horses and mules and from that time on for the rest of the school year I had my nose buried in those books. It got so bad the kids started calling me "Jackass Johnny." But, I learned.

Because of this and the fact that since I was a kid I had worked with horses and mules at home – I started driving a hay rake when I was five or six – I took an interest in the livestock and Tom Jones' packing operation.

At first, I started going out with Tom and some of the Indian packers working for him. From them I learned the trails, the lay of the land, and most important how to behave in the back country. During those years, I shaped my philosophy of what a guide should be. Anyone can be a packer, learning a few hitches and a trail or two. But, pretty hats and silver spurs don't make a

My wife, Sandy, my brother, Joe Alberta, and one of Sandy's friends in front of the old Jones Store at Beasore. Had it not been replaced, that store would have been more than 100 years old today.

cowboy a guide. It takes something extra to be a true guide.

That is what I wanted to be – a guide service doing those extra things to make my operation special. A guide is a host and a packer, a combination of all that. A guide is supposed to know the country, read Nature's signs, take care of the people he takes out, be able to go out on search and rescue and find someone whether he's afoot or on a horse. He's a mountain man, but more than that, he has got to have a feeling for the environment, the ecology.

(That Johnny achieved that goal is shown clearly by the fact that people from throughout California and all walks of life kept coming back to him year after year because he was special. How special is shown by comments by two members of his family.

(Over the years, Johnny's older brother, Joe Alberta, who died in 1983, and his wife, Gloria, and their five children, were close to Johnny, working with him, training livestock, packing, helping Johnny's wife, Sandy, around the pack station at Mugler Meadow.

(Johnny's feelings for the mountains which he conveyed to customers, family and friends who rode with him were expressed recently by Gloria, "He made the Sierra our backyard. He gave us the mountains and made them feel like home." To this her daughter, Becky Huntsman, added:

("Traveling with other packers was just going some place, fishing or hunting or to a specific camp. With Uncle Johnny, there was the romance of the western atmosphere, a lesson on mountain lore, the history, the landscape. He made the mountains mysterious, an exciting adventure.")

As years went by, I took on more responsibility for Tom Jones' packing operation. By 1935, when I was 17, I was doing it all. Then and later when I was on my own, that is the way I did things.

After that, whenever I met other packers at association meetings or other places, they would ask me, "How come, Johnny, you can get by charging more than we do?"

Sure my prices were higher and whenever others raised their prices, I would go up higher yet, but I told them:

"Come along with us some day, and get out there and wait on these people. Do you take the little kids fishing? Do you bait the hooks for the ladies or clean their fish? If a guy gets a favorite feather fly caught up there in the bush do you take your boots off, climb a tree and take it down?"

"Oh no," they'd say. "We don't do that."

"Well, there you are. You got to be a host. You got to take care of them like an old hen with a bunch of chicks."

Unfortunately in recent years, few seem willing to do that. They'd just take care of their stock. They might help with the cooking and things like that. That's about all, but the industry must do more than that to survive. That's why I prefer the term "guide." In the old days, "packer" was a respected term, but today when someone refers to me as a "packer," some people may ask, "What does he pack, tomatoes, peaches, what?"

Some of the old timers may have been a little rough shod, but they loved the mountains, they took care of their people and the environment. When they spotted a party in for a long stay, say three or four weeks, people like Glen Burns and the Cunninghams, for instance, would "just drop by" every once in a while to make sure everything was o.k. in their camps.

Not long ago, I heard about a packer who spotted a party in the back country and then forgot to come pick them up. The group, a couple of doctors and their wives, waited three days and then had to walk out when they ran out of food.

Commercial packers wonder why they get a bad name. They cause their own problems when they hire untrained kids and send them out with no experience in the mountains, no idea of environment, no idea of good manners. They don't pay the kids anything, the kids don't learn anything and they screw up the landscape. At pack stations, you see beaten up old mangers and dirty troughs half full of mud. It's sickening, and the Forest Service tolerates that. It's a terrible way to serve the public.

When I first started as a guide for Tom Jones, there were three pack stations – Miller Meadow, Jackass Meadow and Beasore. Twenty years later when I went on my own at Mugler Meadow, Miller Meadow had bought out Jackass so there still were three. Now there is only one. Part of the trouble is fewer people are riding, but some pack stations disappeared because they were sloppy, had poor stock, or didn't treat their people or the high country right.

The Forest Service closed one station after a lady got bucked off and broke her back. I recall another had problems with John Barleycorn. The owner's wife hid the booze in the haystack, but he would find it and they would find him upside down in the manger with a horse eating around him. One of the stations changed hands 16 or 17 times since I first went up there.

How did all this look to someone coming for a tour? I've always been funny about how things look and that goes not only for the back country where everything should look nice and natural, the way Nature wants it, but if you are running a good operation, your place needs to look good too, clean, neat, orderly. When I opened my first station at Mugler, I lived in a tent, but it was neat looking, with a floor and everything in place.

People come up here to have a nice time on their vacation. You can't ever have a vacation that is too nice. You could never have a horse that is too nice for them to ride or a saddle that is too nice. When I was active, a lot of cowboys wanted to buy some of my stock and tack.

"They're too nice for dudes," they'd say. Nothing was too nice for my people and I didn't like them to be called "dudes." I never did that. I treated them as family. When anyone working for me complained about an "odd ball," I would tell them:

"Come on, I don't want to hear that. We're all equal in this world. Treat that fellow nice like the rest of them. They can't all be like you and me. Help them with anything. How would you like to go down to their place and have them treat you like an odd ball?"

Guides should remember that this is the customers' party. I see packers who won't stop going up the trail. I got after my guys to tell their parties, "This is your trip. We'll stop when you want to stop. We'll fix your stirrups. If anything hurts, we'll fix it. We want you to get off and rest when you want. This is your trip and we can't make it too comfortable."

For some reason, some young packers today can't seem to handle that.

Remember when foam rubber came out? I got different sized pieces and took it along.

"If you get a little sore" I'd tell the riders, "you can put it in your britches or you can sit on it."

Boy, the women loved it. We'd put it on their saddle or some times they'd shove it in their pants. They would cut a little split so it would help their thighs and knees. Later I saw others doing the same thing. These extra things, like never letting a person on a horse until we had wiped the saddle clean, make the difference between a packer and a true guide. Anybody can pack a mule. That's nothing.

Why I heard about one group of four Girl Scout camp counselors, mostly from the East, who had ridden a lot but never in the back country. In the 1930s, you could hire horses and mules without guides. After their camp at Bass Lake closed, they wanted to take a pack trip on their own, but they didn't know anything about packing a mule.

The pack station operator – it probably was Billy Brown – showed them how to balance the loads and then stood each of them beside a quarter of the mule. While he tied a diamond hitch, he told each of them to remember exactly what he did in their quarter. After that, every time they loaded the mules, that's what they did and got along just fine. That was more than 50 years ago, and I bet every one of them still can tie a quarter of a diamond hitch.

Times are different now, of course, but still the commercial packers and others don't go out of their way enough to help people appreciate and enjoy the back country.

Commercial packers should set the example for all wilderness users, especially those with private stock. I like to see them not get so big that things get out of line. Keep everything neat and clean, show stock users and backpackers how to fit into the environment. They not only should take care of their customers but should help all people, especially backpackers, whenever they can. Many is the time I threw a pack, a bedroll or a tent on the top of a load to help a backpacker who needed it. It might be an old couple or someone with kids who were pooped out or limping or anyone who was having a tough time.

Years ago when I was heading for home after spotting a party in, I caught up with a couple of kids, one big guy about 20 and a little kid about 12 who was limping along. The kid was so tired. He had a heavy pack and big blisters on his feet. I was leading my stock back empty so I gave them a ride. I wouldn't take any money. What I did was nothing. There were others who would have done the same thing. Walt Castle or Bob Barrett, all those people who love Yosemite are "givers." They help people. It's nothing new.

You know the kid grew up to be a big businessman in Fresno and told everyone what I did. A lot of people came to me because of him. Although that's not why you help people, it proves that back country manners and courtesy can be good for business.

People from all over California asked me to guide them because their friends had gone with me and said I was special in how I cared for people and the country. I never advertised. Customers learned about me only by word of mouth. That's how come I packed Nancy and Ronald Reagan when he was governor.

"WHERE MULES WEAR DIAMONDS"
(Johnny Jones Pack Trains Letterhead)

10

The Beginning

When I started taking trips for Tom Jones, he was old and had been packing for a good many years. When younger, he packed out of Bass Lake. Later in the early 1920s, he moved to Beasore to open Madera County's first back country pack station. He had a little store and some campsites too.

It was the end of the road then. Tom, Ella and campers who first went there used to tell about driving into Beasore.

Before the road from Bass Lake to Beasore was built in 1923, they came up the stock trail which we used as late as the 1950s and '60s to move horses and mules from Coarsegold to Beasore and Mugler. We would go up Highway 41 to Road 425C, up Deadwood and across the highway to Thornberry Mountain. We'd cut off to the Golden Ball Ranch on the right, over to Chepo Saddle and then to Sivels, where there was an old apple orchard, and on to Soquel. The old Missouri Ranch had an old apple orchard off to the right on the stock trail, too. They had all kinds of apples, beautiful.

The early campers got along fine in their old cars until they got to Rocky Cut between Soquel and Beasore. That would stop them. It was just a pile of rocks. You could get a team through there, not a big team, but something like a buckboard. They would try to winch those old cars up over the rocks with a block and tackle, but sometimes the car would turn over. I remember one time seeing an old car body there. Someone years ago had just left it.

When I was a kid, we were going up that way when I saw a "dizzy horse." Wherever there was a little flat, people grew their own hay, rye and oats. Shocked the hay with a fork to mature. Then they hauled it into the barn by hand. Most of them didn't have hay balers. I remember the first one I saw. I was riding with Freeman Jones and one other guy up above the ranch a Beasore cousin had up on Road 426. While we were resting, I looked back down about a mile away and said, "Hey, there's a dizzy horse. Look down there, that horse going around and round."

Those two guys cracked up, laughing the whole time I was talking.

"Oh yeah, he's dizzy what do you suppose happened?"

Pretty soon they told me that it was a horse going round on a hay baler. The first old balers, the horse went around and around, the poor thing. I don't know how it worked, but I remember seeing a baler with a big arm that hooked to a singletree on it. I guess it was geared to a plunger that went up and down pressing the hay into bales.

After 1923, when they put in the new road along the present route from Bass Lake to Beasore, it still was a dirt road, but it was pretty good and made it a lot easier on the tourists.

By the early 1930s, Ella was pretty sick and feeble and Tom couldn't leave her much so he showed me the country and taught me what he knew. I did my apprenticeship with him. I learned a lot from him and the Indians who worked with him as guides. Tom was a true mountain man who was a good teacher, one who did things the old ways. Tom didn't want to see any rocks in the kyack to balance the loads, for instance.

"And, we ain't carrying no scales," he'd tell me when he heard some packers weighed their loads. "Your scales are right here in your arms. Balance the loads and match the kyacks up with the same animal each time you move."

I must have been 12 or 13, maybe a little older, but not much, when I took the first trip out by myself as a guide. I was so small, sometimes they had to load and unload the mules for me. Other times I was able to lead the mule up alongside a log and climb up on it and load one side and then turn the mule around and load the other. But, I knew where I was going and how to keep a good camp. I don't remember the name of the people on that first trip, but my

Coming home from my first trip as a guide on my own.

horse was Big Red.

With the exception of 1941 and 1942 when Tom Jones had a relative he wanted to try out, I guided parties for Tom for 20 years. The two years I was not at Beasore, I worked for Jess Rust who ran the stables for Yosemite Park and Curry Company. Jess was the father of Leroy, who was postmaster at Yosemite for so long. He was a prince.

I met a lot of fine people there. I remember when Jess made me wear a tie every time I took out one lady who was staying at the Ahwahnee. All the other guys got after her for stopping or something. She was a real nice lady. I don't remember her name, but I remember she wore a beautiful calfskin vest and the mare she rode was named Laura. I took her out every day for a week and a half. One day she told me, "You are a nice guy, not a blow hard, not hustling me or anything."

Then there was a little bitty tyke who was one of the Schilling family, the spice people. I took her out for every day for a couple of weeks. Mrs. Schilling later told me that other guys who had guided her scolded the girl, "Don't do this. Don't do that." You don't scold a little child.

Another time I took the Belgrano girls, real pretty 16 and 17 year old grand nieces of the Gianninis who had the Bank of America. I rode against them in the Indian Field Days, which were a lot of fun and so colorful, I don't know why they quit it.

They would let the tourists ride the donkeys and compete against the cowboys. We had to get enough cowboys, so they even put cowboy hats and boots on janitors to make them look Western like. The Indians would come full feathered and all, oh man! It was a great show. Mostly it was a gymkhana kind of thing, rescue races and stuff like that. Big guys like Arch Westfall would ride in the rescue races and because I was so light I was the one to be picked up. That way they would win.

For Indian Field Days, Jess Rust had some nice saddle burros. All the VIPs got those good ones for a bareback-backward burro race. You were sitting facing over the rump going the other way. The Belgrano girls were terrific riders. They rode in San Francisco a lot. Other girls and guys from the cities were competing.

Jess had two colts, two or three years old, spooky little things. You couldn't get on them, but I agreed to try, if I could get on them straight first. The first one went straight out and almost bucked me off. Oh, he bucked and bucked, everybody laughing at me.

"Jess, I can't ride that one backwards," I told him, "let me try the other."

I got on the other okay, and Jess kept saying, "Johnny, that's all right, you

Yosemite's Indian Field Days featured races, colorful Indian costumes, a horse tug-of-war, games and many special events.

(Yosemite Research Library Photos)

14

got to put on a show for them and if you get thrown, that's okay."

Bareback, backwards, my God. There must have been 15 riders lined up, guys, gals and grown-ups on the good donkeys.

"Get smart," I thought to myself. "You used to ride calves and steers and cows."

So I took the rope off the neck and got my leg set up by his wethers and he started bucking. They cut him loose and he started chasing the others because he was behind. He passed a few and it got near the finish line, about a mile from the stable, so I hit him with the end of the rope and he passed them all, headed for the barn. I rolled off and he went clear to camp and I never saw him again and I'm glad.

One of the Belgrano girls came over and I was all covered with leaves and dirt, and said, "Hey, shy guy. How come you beat me? I had the best donkey."

"Mine just headed for the stable," I said. She invited me over to the Ahwahnee and all the guys wanted me to take her to a dance at Mather that night, but I never saw her again.

Before and after I was in Yosemite, there were other pack stations near

A stop at Nevada Falls while working as a guide in Yosemite.

Beasore, but people from Fresno and Madera Counties kept coming back to us. Of course, when I was a little kid, before I started to take out pack trips, I had worked and played with their kids and we were friends, but the main reason they kept coming back was because I did things a little differently.

After Ella died, my foster father married Hilda Black, who had been the wife of the game warden and a friend of the family for years. It was Hilda who made Jones Store in Beasore famous for its hamburgers and food. She's a lovely lady.

With Tom getting older, they became less interested in the packing operation. I couldn't afford to buy them out or buy any other pack station, which I thought you had to do to get a permit. So, at the end of the 1952 season, I told people I was going to work for the Yosemite Park and Curry Company or Yosemite National Park the following year.

"Oh no, Johnny, you've packed us, our kids and our friends for 20 years," they told me. "You belong here. You can't do that. We don't want you to go."

In the spring of 1953, I started getting calls from all over California. They told me to be home on a certain day, a group was coming to see me. I didn't know what was up, so I was a little shaky when five or six cars pulled up. Some were people I had packed out like the insurance man Ben Knapp, Fresno County Recorder Ike Farley and Arch Shaw who owned the Raymond Telephone Company and some I didn't know. I couldn't believe it. Anyway we went to Yosemite. They left me in a room and went in to a meeting with the Park superintendent, Mr. John C. Preston, a super guy. Pretty soon he came out and said, "Johnny you've got to keep up the good work. John Bingaman (he was the ranger in the south end then) and others have watched you for years, cleaning up other peoples' camps and packing it out. Just keep up the good work. We need you here in the Park."

I just bawled. That's how I got my own permit to pack in Yosemite's back country.

My first pack station was at Mugler Meadows on 40 acres of private land I got from Eldon and Nellie Behney of Lemoore. I'd first met Mrs. Behney when I was just a kid at Beasore. She and her daughter, Mrs. Stanley Hiten of Oakhurst, came through with a bunch of kids headed for the Devil's Postpile. They must have had 20 head of stock with them. When they stopped to camp at Jones Store, one of their horses was lame, but the cowboys around the store wouldn't shoe it for her. I got upset with them.

"I shod a horse or two and have helped." I told Tom. "I can do it. I feel sorry for that poor lady stranded over here with a lame horse."

I took a big rope and tied up the mare's leg and shod the horse while she kicked and kicked. Matter of fact, I got a brand where she ran a nail right through my hand. Mrs. Behney thanked me. When I wouldn't take any money, she said, "The good Lord will take care of you for helping us."

I found out later Mrs. Behney was quite a lady who would round up a bunch of kids and take them on pack trips to the mountains. She was something. Years later when I was starting on my own, the family came to me and said they had bought 40 acres at Mugler, plus another 80 and had logged both. Now they would sell me the 40 for just what they paid for it, which wasn't much. That's how I got started.

John C. Preston
Yosemite Superintendent
(Yosemite Research Library Photo)

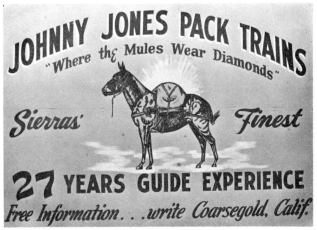

The Mugler Meadow pack station "Where the Mules Wear Diamonds." Home was a tent with a floor. Only a tarp kept out wind on two sides of the kitchen, where my mother's old wood and propane stove served us well, and the picnic table "dining room." The tack room was the only building. The corral was built of logs.

While working for Tom, I had bought a few head of my own stock and some tack when I had a few extra dollars. As soon as I was on my own, I built up slowly. I always was particular. As I kept adding, instead of buying five horses or mules, I'd buy two good ones. Starting out with 10 or 15 head of stock, I could have had twice that number, but I always wanted quality rather than quantity. I never got beyond 40 or 42 head of stock — get too big and it gets out of hand. The most I ever had were two or three guides working for me, all people who liked to tour. It was service, not size, that mattered. I wanted to have control of the people and to keep my parties to select groups, so I charged more.

When I was growing up with Tom, I saw the problems in the back country. A guide will make or break you. It was hard to find good guides who would act more like hosts than a cowboy kind of a guy who would get a little sloppy. They were taking away from nature, spoiling it. My crew had to set an example of how we are supposed to fit into the environment, clean cut, young guys from nice families, all spiffed up, polite and with good personalities. I didn't want any windy guys who did all the talking. You learn more listening all your life.

Some of my guys had worked with horses; some had not. It didn't make too much difference. Those who hadn't sometimes worked harder to learn. You can teach a guy or a gal who has been around stock a little bit, but not really enough to set things in his head too much. If they come with what their grandpa or their daddy told them, it's hard to move them because they have those old ideas. If he's got it in him and he's open minded, wants it bad enough and loves the mountains, he'll make it whether he grew up with stock or not.

When they first came, they were put on a detail of picking up papers and cleaning camp, just the way I started out. If they had it in them, were athletic, had class and were neat, they would go with me on an extended trip. That's the way to train them. Explain it to them, let them see how you do it. They pick it up better than just telling them. After a couple of years, when they were 18, they would have a trip of their own, but I'd go along to see how they did. If they were capable, they'd be turned loose with a bunch of people.

Even my four nephews, Joe and Gloria Alberta's kids, all of whom are excellent stockmen, started out this way as did several others including Wayne Tex who grew up with horses and turned out to be a fine ranch manager. They had to do that type of apprenticeship before taking tours on their own.

It was not only the guides who had to be trained, but the people who toured. I went with as many as possible so I could sort of govern things, educate the kids and the people. Even the grown-ups didn't know what was right.

Training all stock users about back country manners was important then and still is. Even when I met people with private stock, I kind of explained to them in a nice way, "These are our mountains and we got to take care of them. If you don't, I'll have to come to your camp because we have to cooperate with the rangers and keep it nice for the next guy."

As I mentioned earlier, one pack station in our area was closed down because the Forest Service took the permit away when someone got hurt. I'm proud to say that I never had an accident. But, to have a perfect record of no accidents, you have to have good stock and pay attention and communicate with the people you are guiding.

If you have a good safety record and serve as a guide should, the word gets around even without advertising. Even while working for Tom, people from Southern California and the San Francisco Bay area began to call me for tours. There were a lot from San Jose, including the mayor who packed out several times. These were professional people, doctors, engineers, attorneys and such. Groups like insurance company executives, electronics firm people, friends and families would go on tours. There were a few celebrities, the first of whom was Edgar Rice Burroughs and his wife who I took into Spotted Lake. I didn't know they were famous until I came home.

Fibber McGee and Molly, whose real names were Marian and Jim Jordan, went with me for eight years until Marian got real sick. They loved the mountains even though Marian was real spooky about bears. Jim had a beautiful voice. Evenings around the campfire, I'd play my harmonica and he'd sing up a storm. Stewart Hamlin and Bart McLain went with me several times. I remember Bart played kind of a tough guy in the movies, but he was real nice. He owned a ranch down between Coarsegold and Raymond.

Bart McLain and a retired Hollywood stunt man, Chad Trower, tried to get me to be a movie cowboy, but I wouldn't give up my beautiful mountains, especially after one trip to L. A. It was winter and I was through packing when Bart talked me into driving a truck down there to help bring some things back to his ranch. I'm not a good truck driver and I don't like cities. I'll never forget Sepulveda Boulevard. I thought we'd never get through it, but we did and ended up in a big house on a hill in Los Angeles somewhere. It had at least four telephones.

That night we all went to dinner in a big fancy eating place and met all those old movie stars, Bob Steele, Dick Foran, Big Boy Williams, Leo Carrillo and a whole bunch of guys. The meal was great, but they got to partying. I

Fibber McGee and Molly in camp.

thought we'd all end up in jail, so I went out and sat in the car. We finally got back to the house and I wanted to go home to Coarsegold the next day, but they weren't feeling so good. We were there a week and they partied every night. I stayed home and ate what was in the ice box, which was a big one, I'm glad to say.

When some of those guys and Slim Pickens, an old, old friend, suggested I become a movie cowboy, I just had to remember that trip if I ever had any such ideas, which I didn't.

I turned down a chance to ride the year-around professional rodeo circuit for the same reason, I didn't want to give up the High Sierra. I liked rodeoing. When I was probably three or four, Mr. Bundy, my neighbor over in Patterson who first took me to Beasore, thought it was the funniest thing to lift me up and put me on a Billy goat and watch him buck. He'd laugh and laugh. That was my first experience at bareback riding.

Later when we were a little older, us kids didn't have Little League or other things to do so we would go out in a farmer's field and when he wasn't looking, snub a heifer or a steer to a tree. One of us would get on him and then they'd cut us loose. It was good fun.

Over at Hildreth on the Bigelow Ranch, they held a rodeo every year and a lot of the big time cowboys got their start there when they were young. All of us kids rode over there. When I was 18 or 20, some of the guys said, "Come on, let's go professional. We can ride as well as those guys." So I went and rode mostly in California and Arizona, but only during the off season for packing.

Frank Snyder jumped me down south at one rodeo. Snyder was a world champion and I think he's in the Hall of Fame. It was a three-day show and he bucked off this big bull after he rode him a ways. I rode the same bull later and he did a job, almost got me. I was zig-zagging and I ran him over by the fence. I rode him further than Snyder and I went over the fence faster than he did, too.

When I bucked off, Snyder came over and said, "Hey, kid, why don't you come with me? We'll teach you a little more. We'll teach you to ride bareback horse."

No, I told him. I didn't like bareback horse for one thing. I had enough bucking horses when I was a kid, breaking colts for five dollars a month, but most of all I didn't want to leave the mountains.

I remember one time Wilbur Plaugher, who used to come to the Hildreth rodeo when he was a kid, was clowning for a big night show. I rode this one bull, I think his name was "Squarehead" or something like that. When I got off, he said, "My God, that bull only been rode once or twice. Boy you got it."

Hanging on at the Hildreth rodeo.

Sure enough I won the money that day, but most of the time you just donated because you got bucked off.

I rode professional for eight or 10 years, maybe a little more, but I never rode around the clock, went in spurts and jerks just when I felt like it. I was packing in the summer, so I would rodeo only in the spring or fall, maybe only a month or two each year. I did it just for fun. Mostly bulls. I liked a bull. You are supposed to grab him and ride him anyway you can. I was fluid and had balance, I guess. I had some strength in my shoulders and arms, but was not that strong in my legs. I was never one of those who could grab a horse with his spurs and stay on top.

It was just a crazy fun thing to do as a kid, but I "donated" a lot of time on the ground.

The one good thing about that trip to Hollywood and my rodeo experience, the word about my pack operation got around Hollywood. Slim Pickens probably was responsible for it at the start. He grew up in Hanford and long before he got in the movies he had a little saddle horse and pony ring at the Forks at Bass Lake. We both rode in those old informal rodeos on the Bigelow Ranch at Hildreth.

My most famous guest, then Governor Reagan, insisted on Johnny Jones as a guide because of the advice of an old friend of his who had gone with me years before.

I had sold out at Mugler and Soldier Meadows and was concentrating on buying, selling and breeding mules, just taking tours for special friends. I wasn't guiding that much when I got a call from Bob Barnett, one of the finest stockmen ever, who was running the Curry stables. I had taken a few specials for him in the past, but turned him down this time.

"You got 30 guys working there that can take a party," I told Bob. "I can't do it. I have something else cooking."

Then a couple of nights later here came a couple of calls from Movie Corporation of America people down south. MCA owned Curry then. The answer still was "No," but it got me thinking. So when Bob called again and said, "You just got to take this one. You won't regret it," I broke down and agreed. I didn't know what it was all about.

The Curry people came to Mugler and scouted around looking for an out of the way road where limousines still could get in. We picked out a little spur way back in from main roads, but near a trailhead. Seemed like kind of a hideout. Kind of spooky. Curry brought the stock and supplies over to Mugler. We took the saddle horses to the end of the road and went back for the pack animals which had been loaded early in the morning, leaving the tops open for personal items. While we were taking the mules over, I heard a little noise and turned to look back and here came two big, long limousines. The windows were dark so all I could see was the shape of someone waving. We pulled off and let them go by. I wondered if it was someone from the Mafia.

I didn't know who it was until we got up to the trailhead where the horses were and saw security guards and that kind of western hat I had seen Governor Reagan wear on television. The party consisted of Nancy Reagan and her aide, Nancy Reynolds, a real nice lady who owned a resort on the Salmon River in Idaho; the governor's son, Ronnie, Jr.; Norman "Ike" Livermore, the state resources head; his wife and two security guards. Sam Livermore, "Ike's" son, was working for the Curry Company at the time and came along as a packer. Lloyd Light, a good hand, was the cook.

The security guards were okay, but they brought along some pretty big weapons for some reason. I don't know what they were, but they were packed in several large, long cases. When we were packing the last minute items at the trailhead, Sam and I had to struggle to get those things in just right wondering how fast we could unpack the mules and get the weapons if they were needed.

Not long ago, Sam reminded me about the care with which he and I

The packers responsible for Governor Reagan's trip to the Yosemite wilderness, left to right, Bob Barnett, head of the Park and Curry Company stables, myself, Lloyd Light and Sam Livermore.

constructed a special seat, a "biffy," out of some boards we found at the first camp. We even rounded and smoothed the edges with a horseshoeing rasp. Mrs. Reagan was not used to camping and how things were out in the backcountry. It was welcomed.

We took them through Chiquito Pass, into Chain Lakes and on to Moraine Meadows where we stayed for two or three days with side trips to Givens Lake and Big Breeze Lake. It was beautiful. On the way out to Yosemite Valley we stopped at Illilouette then dropped down to Nevada Falls and on to the stables at the Valley floor where we were met by the limousines. Coming down from the falls, I was leading the group and got a surprise when the security people stepped out of the bushes in front of me. They sure were on the job.

Governor Reagan was a real nice fellow in camp, just like you and me. He just loves the mountains, loves horses, loves people. I was really impressed by the way he talked to all the kids he saw on the trail. He'd tell them he liked to see young ones in the mountains because the mountains are good for them. And, he'd tell them, "They're your mountains, so take good care of them."

He was willing to work, go out and do things for you. And, he was tough too, rugged and woolly. One day way down below camp at Moraine Meadows, I was going down checking horses and I saw him out in a pool in the South Fork of the Merced River. Ten o'clock in the morning. The sun was out, but it still was pretty cold.

"God," I said to him, "it's too cold to take a bath. What are you doing?"

"Just enjoying the clean, cool mountain water."

He didn't have soap, towel, nothing. Pretty soon he came out in the bushes. Tough son of a gun.

When I tour, I always watch a fellow or a girl at first. If by the end of the day they still are sitting up nice, you know they are good riders. The governor was a terrific rider. Going into Breeze Lake there is a lot of rock and some slick rock, but he didn't find it so bad, so we rode right up to about 50 yards from the lake. He stood, took some pictures and said, "How lucky you guys are up here, breathing this air, relaxing."

Sam, Lloyd and I had our camp away from the Reagans' party, but one night Nancy Reynolds came over and insisted we join them around their campfire.

"Johnny Jones, you know something," the governor said. "You packed some dear friends of mine several years ago. Do you remember a group of five or six young people who were studying to be in the ministry?"

I did. That had to have been 30 years earlier. I stayed with them for a week. Real nice young guys. Well, one of them was the governor's minister, Rev.

Lewis Evans.

"Gosh John," Governor Reagan said, "You showed them such a nice time and they talked about you, so. . ."

I found out later from friends that he had checked the whole State of California, so he had a choice. Ike Livermore had worked for some packer over on the east side but the governor tracked me down and that's why Bob Barnett insisted I had to go. Bob was right. It was worth it. It was an honor.

RONALD REAGAN
GOVERNOR

$\mathfrak{State\ of\ California}$
GOVERNOR'S OFFICE
SACRAMENTO 95814

July 16, 1973

Mr. Johnny Jones
Valley Stables
Yosemite Park
Curry Company
Yosemite Village, California 95389

Dear Johnny:

My family and I want you to know how much we enjoyed your good company on our recent pack trip into the Sierra. I was certainly impressed by your hard work and good nature. It was a rare experience for all of us, and we only wish it had been longer.

Again, Johnny, many thanks for all that you did to make our trip so comfortable.

Sincerely,

RONALD REAGAN
Governor

Dams, Bridges & Things

Life in a pack station wasn't always riding through beautiful high wilderness country with friends and celebrities.

No, there were plenty of back-breaking jobs such as supplying materials for dams, bridges or other such projects or long hours tracking and rescuing people who were lost or injured.

One of the toughest jobs we ever tackled was back in 1960, the time that my mules outbid seven helicopter companies.

McClure Lake is up near Isberg Pass, right above Sadler Lake. It is a deep lake that could catch the runoff from the other lakes up above it and feed it into the East Fork of Granite Creek, a beautiful fly fishing stream. In bad years, the creek would run dry and the fish would die. The California Department of Fish and Game, the State Division of Forestry and the U. S. Forest Service got together and decided to put up a dam to raise the lake level and hold back more water until the creek started to run low. Then, they could release it through a big valve and keep the fish alive all year around.

McClure Lake

When they advertised the job of hauling material, food and supplies to McClure, they sent forms to all the packers on the east side and the west side of the Sierra; I was the only bidder. The Forest Service people came to me and said, "Well, you got the bid. Nobody else bid it, but there are seven helicopter companies who want to bid."

"That's not fair, bidding a mechanized deal against an animal," I insisted. "You don't want those choppers back in that nice country."

The government people said they were afraid they were going to have to do it and fooled around and went to bid again. I bid against them and got the job at a little over $1 per 100 pounds less than any helicopter company, as I recall. There were times that summer when I wished the helicopters had got the contract.

That was tough, but we got the job done. We packed 44 tons of cement, dynamite, compressors, fresh food for a big crew, reinforcing steel, drill steel, wheel barrows, everything you could think of all out of Soldier Meadow. Sixteen miles uphill. Thank God we didn't have to take too much sand from Soldier Meadow as we were able to get most of it from a bar in Sadler Lake just below McClure.

We got a lot of publicity, though. Different friends would call, camera hunters from Piedmont, Lafayette and all through the San Francisco Bay area. They heard about it when the Oakland Tribune ran a little cartoon entitled "Mules Best Helicopters." It showed a group of mules climbing up a steep cliff with a helicopter down below looking up at them. Underneath the caption read:

"Gee, Haw! Pack mules beat out helicopters for Fish and Game Department construction job in the High Sierra. Johnny Jones Pack Trains bid a job at $5.50 per 100 pounds against the helicopters' second low bid of $6.67."

The cement was the trickiest. They were in 90 pound sacks, two to a mule. One hundred and eighty pounds is a good load for a mule. I talked to some of the old timers and started out with regular kyacks — bags which swing from each side of the pack saddle. I soon found it would take something special to do the job. The cement sacks, sitting low on the side of the mule, would knock the mule's ribs. When they were puffing hard, it would knock them out. We had to do something different.

For several years I had guided professors from the veterinary school at U. C. Davis and listened when they talked about livestock. They also invited me to many of their clinics so I had learned a lot about mules, their lungs, how they breathed and how to keep them healthy.

Thinking it over, I figured we had to get those loads higher up on top of the

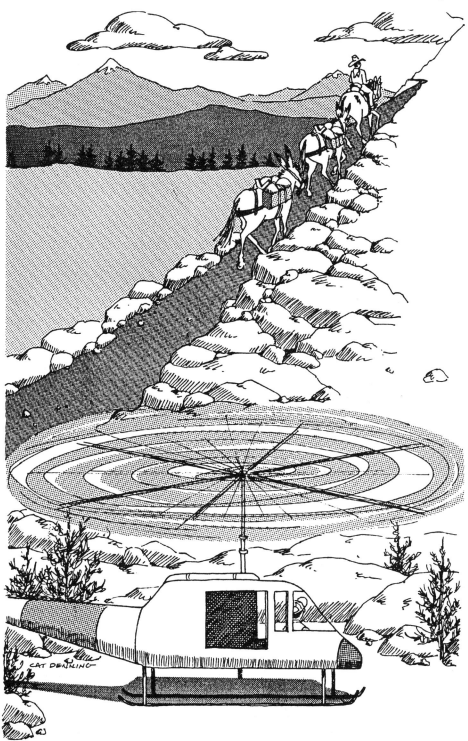

mules to help their lungs. So, I went down to a canvas shop in Fresno and paid extra for them to jump on the job real quick to make special pack bags. They were heavy, real heavy, duck canvas kyacks with a low back so the cement sacks would have a little room around them. The kyack straps were made so you could slap the kyack way up high on the forks of the pack saddle. The cement sacks would stick up a little bit and come together so you could tie the cement bags together at the top of the saddle. This way you could get air under the load and protect the mules' backs. Then we put a little flap on the kyacks so we could protect the cement if it happened to rain. It worked perfectly. No sore backs because we could keep them clean and treat their backs with sulphur which worked better than washing them off with salt as some people do.

The mules were loaded at the end of the road at Soldier Meadow. We built long ramps, 200 to 300 feet long, where the trucks unloaded. The packers would bring the mule strings right in to the ramps, like in a chute, so they wouldn't have to lift that weight too high. Some of them still had to moan and groan to get the loads up on those big mules.

When we packed in the material for the Miller Bridge across the Middle Fork of the San Joaquin River, we had to pick everything right up off the ground where the trucks unloaded at the end of the road. It wasn't that much, but it would just kill you, especially a little guy like me lifting up against those big, husky packers. So the ramps were pretty nice.

Although the distance was short from Sadler Lake to the dam site, only about a mile, packing the sand posed another problem — loading and unloading. For this I had airplane aluminum kyack boxes made with a trap door on the bottom. Pull a little lever and the box would empty itself without lifting the boxes off the mule. Flop the bottom back up, put the levers back and go load it again. To load, the mules went into a little trench at the sand bar at the edge of the lake so the guys wouldn't have to lift the sand too high. They would fill five-gallon cans, heave them up and empty them into the special boxes. That way the loads would balance. Worked great. They just kept going. Never took the boxes off. You had to have gentle mules though. They had to get used to the bottom dump thing and not spook.

One string did nothing but carry food in every other day. There was a big crew there, must have been at least 20 or more, including the California Youth Authority kids, Fish and Game, Forest Service, Division of Forestry people plus I don't know how many others, including visitors and inspectors we had to take in. They fed well, lots of meat, fresh fruit and vegetables, fresh milk and everything else. With food runs and rotating pack animals, we had 30 mules going in every day. The strings would leave in the morning for the uphill trip. At the dam, they would unload, feed the mules some grain and head downhill at night, a 32 mile round trip.

We had plenty of mules and treated them right. We were lucky because I had been shipping mules in from Missouri, Arkansas and those states and I had a lot of extra mules. At Soldier Meadow, I built a huge kind of round corral, just like a wheel. The hay stack was at the hub so all the mules had hay out in front of them all the time. The spokes formed good sized pens in which each packer kept his own stock. There was a nice big meadow with a stream going through it. Water was piped to troughs, good fresh water for each group of mules. They could eat or lay around when not working. When one got a little fatigued, we let him rest for three or four days. We had plenty of mules.

Each packer had about six mules in a string plus three horses he could rotate. Nobody else could touch them. He had his own regular stock, plus the relief stock which he could use whenever he wanted to rest his regular string. I watched them all pretty close. If I saw he should rest one, I would insist, even if the packer said he was doing o.k.

"Just let him rest, he deserves it. We got a lot of mules," I'd tell him.

When we assigned the mules to the packers, the big leggier ones went to the taller guys and the little ones to guys like me.

Mules we had, but we had problems keeping packers, especially toward the end of summer and the start of fall. Even though we paid triple the regular wage and fed packers and their wives, some of them couldn't hack it. One guy from over Bishop quit almost at once. I know it was a killer, but when one quit

McClure Lake Dam is completed.

31

The first mules to go across the new Miller Bridge.

it really put a load on you.

Although some of the guys pulled out, we had good people who stayed with us. I recall especially my old friend Wayne Tex, now a ranch manager over in Bishop, Lewis "Bud" Shannon, a big, tall fellow from down Raymond way, and Clyde Connel who came out from Arizona to work for us. He was tough.

These guys stayed with me all the way, but as the summer turned to fall, more of the others dropped out. What saved my bacon then was Bob Barnett over at the Yosemite Park and Curry Company. At the end of his season in the Park, Bob offered to come over with his mules. They were in good shape, out of work and he would just have to turn them loose. So he and two of his best men came over to help. We got it all in there before the snows came.

Construction of the Miller Bridge, pretty well up the Middle Fork of the San Joaquin River in what now is the Ansel Adams Wilderness, wasn't nearly as tricky.

We packed everything in but the big steel beams which were flown in by choppers. Matter of fact, they lost one of those beams. Caught in a down draft, the helicopter almost crashed and had to drop it. It's still down there some place. We packed in plywood, form lumber, cement, rebar, sand, food, wheel barrows, compressors, steel bolts, lots of bolts — everything else that was needed. It all was packed from McCreary Meadow, a long nine miles downhill. In some ways, it's tougher on mules going down hill with heavy loads which tend to push up on their shoulders and the mules have to brace themselves all the time. The trail wasn't that good either, pretty sandy in spots and bad rock in others. We would lead them in, but coming out empty was duck soup. We'd turn them loose and head for home. It took a season and a half to do the job. Bud Shannon started with me in the fall of 1957 and then Wayne took it all the following summer.

It was the kind of job that made packing an art and both those guys, Bud and Wayne were good. I doubt that many of the pack station operators could handle either of those jobs today, especially continuing our regular guide service which we kept up along with those big jobs. So many of today's packers never learned the art. As I have said before, it's no business for candlestick makers or hobbyists.

The "packer" always has been a respected profession of people who could move all types of equipment into places where only mules could go.

I think, especially, of packers like Glen Burns of Clovis, one of the greatest old timers. Years ago, when he had a pack station in the Huntington Lake district, he packed compressors, generators and other heavy equipment into remote Southern California Edison powerhouse projects. Imagine, some of those loads weighed more than 500 pounds. Some of the old timers packed tandem, using two mules with two big timbers stretching one each side of both mules. The heavy load was hung between them. That worked okay if you didn't have sharp switchbacks. Years ago I saw where someone tried to pack a compressor tandem going down into the San Joaquin River. What happens, if the shafts are low, they get caught in a tight switchback. The front mule scoots the other one over the edge. The back mule went over the cliff dragging the load and the other mule with him, compressor and all down into the bottom of the canyon. It's tough.

Glen Burns knew some tricks. He used a special tandem rig. He had what he called a shoe or a plate that sat on top of the pack saddle. It would turn or tip so the shafts would sit as high or higher than the level of the mules' backs so there was clearance when they made a sharp turn. I never tried packing tandem, but Bob Barrett, who still is an active packer for Yosemite Park, told me that Walt Castle, retired head of the Park Service stables, used to pack 20-foot lengths of pipe that way.

"A mule back there and a mule up here." Bob explained. "The pipe laid up high on swivels. Lead one mule and the other stayed back there. They'd work together and when they came to a switchback the load would swivel like a fifth wheel. He would have a little trouble once in awhile, but he made it go."

In "Yosemite, Where Mules Wear Diamonds," his fascinating history of Yosemite's packers, mule shoers, teamsters and trail workers, Barrett shows pictures of his mules carrying two 14-foot steel stringers for back-country bridges. One beam on each side, it added up to a 300 pound load. Barrett, who also teaches horse management, history of people and animals in the Sierra and other courses at Merced College, includes photos of a heavy iron cook stove, a high country outhouse and a 300-pound stone boat being loaded on the backs of mules. Years ago, they tell me, long pieces of lumber were packed so that one end stuck out over the head of the mule and the other end was rather low to the ground.

Another skill in which all true mountain men, and especially packers, should excel is search and rescue. Sometimes that involves tricky packing techniques in order to get injured people out of the high country without hurting them more. Not all the searches turned out well, unfortunately, as I have had to pack out two or three dead people.

For centuries, the backs of mules have been the only way that heavy items, whether they are generators, cannons and other war material, timbers, food and supplies, compressors, cement, injured people or any of a lot of other heavy loads, can be carried in the high mountains.

Genghis Khan's fierce riders get the credit for ruling much of Europe and Asia, along about the year 700, but these wild men were supplied by livestock loaded and driven by probably the finest packers the world has ever known. Generations of army generals, as recently as World War II, kept their troops supplied by men driving mules and horses. The U. S. Army's 10th Mountain Division, where Bud Shannon from Coarsegold served during World War II as a packmaster, had 3,000 mules. Matter of fact, it was only 15 or 20 years ago that the Norwegian Army gave up a specially bred, small, strong packhorse and switched to jeeps.

George Washington, Lewis and Clark and thousands of other explorers relied on the ingenuity and talents of packers and their mules. Today they are the only legal way to haul heavy material into designated American wilderness areas.

True packers are the only ones who have the knowledge to see that the loads are balanced right, know how to pack special, odd shaped, heavy loads and insure the mules and horses are kept healthy and safe. There may be better ways of making money, much better. It is hard work, even if you have been at it for years and have been around those old buzzards who shared their secrets with you sometimes, if they got to know and like you.

In order to make it, you have to know that's the life you want and be willing to get better and better at it every day as long as you live. To maintain stock in the back country is no monkey business. It's something that you do only because you really love it. I wouldn't have had it any other way. I couldn't have done anything else. It's a profession which should not be allowed to die.

Cinching up.

A long string.

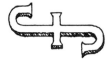

Sixty Years of Change, Good & Bad

In more than a half century of riding through the back country of Yosemite National Park and adjoining National Forests, the changes I have seen have been dramatic.

Not only have the number of visitors skyrocketed, but the manner in which people approach and treat the areas now designated as wilderness is different. Some of the changes are good. Some not. And, there are other changes that should be made.

In the early 1930s, while barely in my teens, I started working as a guide. Relatively few people traveled the back country then. Most of those who did venture into the High Sierra rode horses with mules to carry the loads. They had little choice. Sleeping bags and bedrolls weighed pounds instead of the ounces counted today. No camp cook would be without a cast iron Dutch oven and griddle. All the rest of their gear was heavy too. The ardent fisherman who hiked in for a weekend usually led a donkey or mule to carry his gear. If he was husky enough to pack it himself, it was on a heavy wood and canvas backpack.

With the dramatic development of today's featherweight backpacking equipment, foods packed especially with weight in mind, tiny stoves and all types of other special lightweight equipment and construction of more forest roads for access, the wilderness has been opened to thousands. Overnight stays in Yosemite Park wilderness areas alone number 70,000 or more each year. That's good, because it is important that people enjoy the High Sierra so long as they take care of it.

Looking back on nearly 60 years of living in the Sierra high country, it's not the great increase in numbers of people that worries me, but the way people do things.

Most stockmen and backpackers I know love the mountains and talk about protecting the wilderness. The Park, God bless, doesn't allow hunters and the amount of hunting in National Forests seems to be decreasing. More people go to the back country to fish, to hunt with a camera or just for the solitude and relaxation. You find more environmentally-oriented people in the high country. They mean well, but still there is more abuse. Mostly, it's caused by just plain ignorance of how to behave in the back country.

I suppose it isn't surprising that people who grew up in the city where street sweepers and garbage trucks pick up their trash don't think about dropping toilet paper, cigarette butts, gum and candy wrappers and worse. These are just some of the things that many backpackers and stock users do today because they just don't seem to know better. There may be plenty of books about how to behave in the wilderness, but I guess too many people don't read.

There's going to be no true wilderness left if we don't start educating people. We have to get in on the ground floor and start with the kids in school. Somehow, they have to be taught, and I challenge both the back country stock user associations and the backpacking organizations to meet their responsibilities to educate wilderness users to change their ways and protect, instead of abuse, the high country.

Because I have lived and worked with livestock all my life, I find myself most critical of abuse caused by some private owners of horses and mules as well as some commercial packers, even though together they make up only two or three percent of high country users.

One positive change made recently is the limit on the number of stock that can go in a single party. Yosemite and the National Forests around it have agreed to limit livestock use to 25 head per party with a limit of 15 people. Some in the packing business may not agree with me, but I think that's plenty. Both Yosemite Park and the National Forests should enforce the limits on hiking groups too. They have a limit of 15 in wilderness areas, but I have seen 50 or 60 backpackers in a group. I've talked to some of them, but most of them didn't want to talk. I'm sure they just slipped in without permits.

Before my time, I understand Sierra Club parties into the high country would require 100 head of stock or more. Even when I started in, the club was sponsoring trips nearly that large. Can you imagine what that did to the meadows and trails and the rest of the country?

I do recall when I was a kid I saw some old time guides lead parties with 40 or 50 head of stock. They wouldn't go in and hit one certain spot but would move on and tour around several places. These guides were good people such as Glenn Burns or Newt Phillips who would take parties all the way from Tuolumne Meadows to Mt. Whitney, spending a month or more on the trail. The Wampler party and the Fuller Brush group were well known trips along these lines.

They would loose herd the pack stock which were all trained to stay in line. Riding through where they were camping you might see some of their people, but you would never see either their camp or their stock. Camps were out of sight, away from streams and meadows. The stock was back up a little canyon. Little gate barriers held the stock well away from the trails and the camps.

When they left you couldn't hardly tell where the livestock or the camp had been. These old timers knew how to handle livestock and keep from damaging the environment, but today things are different. The limits now in force are good.

Banning loose herding, except for one-at-a-time through dangerous spots, also is good. Too many "cowboys" with their big hats and boots would stampede horses and mules down the trail because they had to get to a dance or a date at the bar.

In the last two or three decades more people have acquired "backyard horses and mules." If people know what they are doing, that's fine, but too often a guy goes out and buys a horse and a mule in a sales yard, gets together with a buddy and his animals and heads for the hills. There's going to be trouble. Put animals that are strangers together and they'll get to fighting. Years ago, the old timers ranged their stock together all winter. They ran together like a big old family. They were all buddies. When you got to the high country, all you had to do is hobble one of them and the rest would stay around. They wouldn't leave the leader.

Owners of private stock have to remember that horses and mules are like people. You must treat them right. As Joe Back says in his excellent book "Horses, Hitches and Rocky Trails:"

"Give them hard work, good treatment and plenty of respect and they'll respond in kind. Give them hard work and a dirty deal — you'll get paid in full, sometimes sudden."

For instance, when the day's work is done, you cannot just tie the mules and horses, go have a drink and ignore them. Too often I have seen people leave their animals tied to a picket line or a tree with their packs still on their backs while they go off to do other things.

Although some old-time guides and pack station operators were a bit rough shod, generally they were mountain men who were there solely because they loved the back country. Today there are too few pack stations and too many operators I call "candlestick makers." You know, the butcher, the baker and the candlestick maker. They'll buy a pair of fancy boots and a great big sombrero and without knowing which end a mule feeds, they are supposed to be packers. They come from other professions with little or no real experience or understanding of the mountains. Having a pack station is a hobby for them.

Oh, there are some good guides, but far too few. A guide has to know from A to Z what they are doing, how to be a host, how to take care of the animals, how to treat people. It's just like building a good highway. You get a man who has done it, not one with no brains about highways.

If they get more grass roots people like Bob Barrett to teach, and stock users would listen to them, they will operate the way that will fit in with the environment. Then you'd have something, but too many don't want to listen.

From my observations, the best pack operations and guides are those close to Yosemite National Park. That's because the Park Service and the Curry Company packers under people like Bob Barnett of Curry Company and Bob McGregor and Walt Castle for the government set an example that forced nearby pack outfits to upgrade their stock, tack and operations. Bob Barnett and Jess Rust, when they ran the Curry Company stables, insisted on a class operation. It was all politeness and neatness, no ragtag stuff. Anyone who didn't go along went down the road in a hurry.

Too many stock owners and backpackers don't understand "back country manners." This leads to the major change which I believe should be made in managing the wilderness. Both the commercial and the private stock owner, as well as the backpacker, should be tested by the Park Service and the Forest Service before they are issued wilderness permits.

Sure it would be a tough job, but it would help protect the wilderness and cut down on search and rescue. Everybody involved, the stock user, the hiker and the rangers themselves, must be better educated in how to care for the high mountains. If we don't, they won't be nice for our grandchildren and their children.

Ideally, I would hope that both agencies would set up clinics to test commercial stock operators every two or three years in order to renew their permits. They should come with their animals and show what they can do. Let them perform. Let them give a demonstration of what they are going to do in the back country. I'd want them to load up, go 100 yards and see how they unpack. Owners should be responsible for making sure their packers are qualified too.

Private stock owners should be tested every year before they get a wilderness permit. Along with commercial operators, they should be made to show they know how to picket or hobble, how to load to insure that the packs ride properly without causing sores or injuries to the animal and generally how to care for their stock.

I'd hold clinics for backpackers, too. On-the-ground tests or clinics should teach backpackers and private stock users how and where to set up camp, how to prevent fires and water pollution, how to keep the environment clean and pure and how not to get lost.

I'd give clinics for stock users every year in the Spring, right there at North Fork, at Yosemite Park stables and other central locations They might even

Packers like Bob McGregor (bottom) and Walt Castle (top) of Yosemite could carry about anything on the backs of mules. *(Yosemite Research Library Photos)*

41

hold clinics as part of Mule Days in Bishop. After all, Mule Days were organized to help improve the quality of the care and handling of livestock, tack and the back country.

Let them talk about the back country. Fire some questions at them to find out what they know. If they're knowledgeable, okay, but get a little more input into them. That will make them better. They should love that. A good person wouldn't mind coming back every year, and a bad person needs the training.

Administratively, both the Park Service and the Forest Service tell me it would be a tremendous headache. I think protecting the back country is worth it.

If they cannot do this, the least that could be done would be to make every wilderness permit applicant take a test. I mean hikers as well as stock users. It could be simple. A small booklet, an expansion of the information sheets that already go out when permits are issued, could be sent with application forms. These would cover the rules and regulations of wilderness use and back country manners. A one or two page test like that the Department of Motor Vehicles gives for a driver's license or the State Department of Boating and Waterways sends with its boating safety course would be completed and returned before a wilderness permit would be issued.

By returning the test papers, which they probably will answer while looking at the booklet, you will know they at least opened the book.

I know that today both the National Parks and the National Forests have more rangers connected with the wilderness than they once did. That's good. Most rangers are young, college-trained, environmentally-oriented, good people who mean well, but budget restrictions coupled with the impact of the number of wilderness visitors reduce their effectiveness. They still are too few and overwhelmed with work.

The Park has done a better job in the back country because its people work the field. The Forest Service is a little lax. They aren't back there that much and I don't think they really are up to date on how to operate in the wilderness. The Forest Service has rules, but they don't live by them. The rules for commercial packers say: "You cannot have chronic back or any other problems nor abuse stock." But, there has been so much stock abuse back there. The Forest Service lets anyone get a pack station permit, they don't check on his background and these people are serving the public.

In earlier days, rangers and wilderness visitors had natural mountain sense. They were true environmentalists, although at that time that term hadn't been invented. Today, unfortunately, while many want to help the environment, they lack mountain sense. No matter how much a young fellow or girl who came out here because they wanted to get away from the city may love the mountains, you cannot put them out as a wilderness ranger without some basic training in what the back country is all about.

Wilderness managers should spend more time in the back country, and they should ride and work with stock. If trails are good for stock they will be good for foot pounders. Top administrative people used to get out into the back country just to keep in touch; talk with people and see what's really going on. They went with a patrol ranger or two and not big groups. Now paperwork seems to keep them tied to a desk. When they do get out they tend to go with politically-oriented groups.

Trail work is another area where there are great differences. Trails were better maintained a half century ago with fewer people. Today, both the Park and the National Forest admit they are way behind on trail maintenance. For a while, Park trails were better maintained than those in National Forests, but Park trails aren't as good as they used to be. The trail coming up from Chiquito is bad, for instance, and going into Chain Lakes there is a lot of bad rock. That's dangerous. I used to make tenderfoots walk there, but now it's so bad I won't take people over it even on foot leading a horse.

True, neither agency is given the money to do an adequate job on trails, but

In the old days, patrol rangers traveled the back country as Glenn Fredy is doing here.

Park Superintendent John Preston personally kept in touch with things in the back country. *(Yosemite Research Library Photo)*

too many times what is done is by people who have not been properly trained. Some times I think Park and Forest trail crews don't know how to fix a trail, so they just leave it. Water breaks are important, for instance. The Park used to know how to turn water with rock bars, it's trail crews now are using logs. The Forest Service uses a lot of logs. Logs don't work. Sometimes they don't even use logs, the just dig ditches, not putting in water bars at all. And, how many times have I seen water breaks channel water across a switchback and right back down the trail rather than divert it. I swear some trail maintenance people don't know water runs downhill.

Years ago, I recall a Forest Service trail crew of just two men, Jack Malone and a man named Shaw. They were rough old codgers. Traveling with a string of maybe 10 or 12 donkeys, all turned loose, they'd be going all summer long. They were quite a sight. Mr. Malone rode in front. He had whiskers so big all you could see were his nose and eyes. Spooky. I wasn't afraid, but I sure tried to be real nice and polite. Mr. Shaw rode on a big donkey in back. They had a great big police dog who always was with Shaw in back.

As years went on I got to know them. They were nice. The jackasses carried everything, including the big cross cut saws lying across the load with the blades pointing backwards. I was fascinated about those burros.

"Mr. Malone," I said one day, "how come my mules and horses want to eat, and yours just don't bother. They just go chit, chit, chit, setting a pace."

"Son, they wouldn't dare to stop to get a blade of grass off to the side," he told me. "See that big dog back there, chase one donk off the trail and he's on him. Trained them donkeys with that dog. The dog will latch on to their faces if they tried to steal grass. They don't leave the trail. They don't pass. They stay in line just like a bunch of ducks."

Every time I met them, I'd look to see if one was out of line. Never! It was beautiful, so pretty going down the trail.

Anyway, whenever they made water bars, they used rocks. These guys were awful good at rockwork in trails. Livestock gets blamed for all trail damage, but a flash rain or melting snow are worse than anything if water breaks are not working properly.

One of the most dramatic changes in treatment of wilderness, both in the Park and the National Forest, has come about because of forest road construction. While designated wilderness areas have remained roadless, new logging and recreation roads have been extended right up to wilderness boundaries. Roads and spurs have opened up areas all through the back country. The result is much easier access, more use and more abuse.

Look what happened when the Forest Service pushed through the timber access road to Quartz Mountain in 1969. It opened up the south end of Yosemite Park. Chain Lakes and surrounding streams and lakes now are among the heaviest used and abused wilderness areas in the Park. They get some pretty rough characters in there and the Park needs to put a ranger at the gate. I've caught hunters with rifles and dogs in as far as Gravely Ford. All I could do was lie and "warn" them a couple of rangers were headed that way.

Sixty years ago, the road from Bass Lake to Beasore was rough and dirty. It didn't go much further than the Meadows. Now it is part of a Scenic Byway loop tying into the Minarets Road out of North Fork. Most of the loop is paved. It and side roads go right up to wilderness boundaries. It may be great that people can look into wilderness areas without getting out of their cars, but somehow that defeats the purpose of wilderness and it increases tremendously the opportunities for uncontrolled access. I have found rough types in the back country who refuse to follow any rules, not even getting permits. This makes it easier for those people who would destroy God's great mountains by abusing them.

One blessing is that they never finished the road across the Sierra from Clover Meadow to Red's Meadow and Devil's Postpile which would have opened up all of what now is the Ansel Adams Wilderness.

Before World War II, the Forest Service built the road into Clover using Civilian Conservation Corps crews. Had it not been for the war, the road would have gone on through. In the late 1950s and 1960s, a move was made to complete the road, then known as Forest Highway 100. Congressmen Bernie Sisk and Bizz Johnson were pushing hard for it and when the Minarets and John Muir Wilderness areas first were established, a corridor was left for the highway. It would have been the only road across the Sierra between Tioga Pass and Walker Pass, a couple hundred miles distant.

I recall in 1959, the California State Chamber of Commerce sponsored a trip following the route. Three of us packers, each with 25 head of stock, took them across. It was a big party, all the big business, trucking and tourism heads from all over the state went. They were all for it, of course.

We had a big storm that night at 77 Corral. I thought we should have stayed over another day, but they had a big meeting scheduled at Mammoth with all the politicians and others who were trying to push the road through, so they voted to go ahead. We hit snow on top and boy it was cold. When we got there, some of them couldn't get out of the saddles by themselves because they were so cold. Some of the men didn't even have boots.

I remember one man who rode a horse of mine named Tony. When he got off, his big shoe caught in the left stirrup and he couldn't get it loose. He stood there kicking and Tony just turned his head and watched him with a disgusted look on his face. Like I say, you got to have select stock. That rider could have been hurt if it hadn't been for a good patient horse.

The storm may have cooled some of their enthusiasm for the road. The party went home by bus after the meetings. As it turned out, there still was a lot of pressure to build the road, but when President Reagan was still governor, the State of California blocked the action. Then, when the Ansel Adams wilderness was created, the corridor was closed. The road never will be built, which is good.

I understand Governor Reagan and Ike Livermore, who was his State Director of Natural Resources, were responsible for the state action. Ike had done some packing on the east side and I guess he talked the governor into looking at the country. Governor Reagan agreed that the Ritter Range country, the Minarets and other areas which once were part of Yosemite Park should be protected and kept wild. This wouldn't have happened if the road had gone through.

One other complete change made in the last few years has been in the ideas the Forest Service has about the importance of history. In many ways the change came too late.

Fifteen or 20 years or so ago, the Forest Service burned a couple of historic old cabins. One, the Knoblock cabin, was located on the Isberg Pass trail four or five miles south of the pass. It was in an area originally in the Park but removed when the boundaries were changed in 1905. I'm sure the cabin was built by cattlemen long before Yosemite Park was created in 1890, so it went way back. Knoblock had the land fenced and raised Timothy hay up there and farmed the place. He even had a cultivator, kind of spring tooth thing pulled by horses. It was a good solid building. Nearby was a big cement and rock root cellar. When it was burned the Forest Service went in and threw all those old farm tools, horse-drawn equipment in the cellar and buried it all.

They did the same thing to the Bugg cabin near Detachment Meadow, along with some others. Someone in the Forest Service got on them about that and they didn't dare touch that little old Chetwood cabin. It's still standing near Detachment Meadow on Chetwood Creek, a tributary to the North Fork of the San Joaquin. Since it is in wilderness, they probably won't do anything to maintain it, so one day it will fall down. Then, the last of those cattlemen's cabins built more than 100 years ago will be gone.

Of course, they made a big thing about the old Hogue Ranch cabin up in the apple orchard above North Fork. The Forest Service moved it and restored it in 1991. When they were done they had all the historians, politicians, supervisors, congressmen, and 200 people or more for a big blowout about saving it.

It's a shame they didn't think about that when they were torching those other cabins.

The Minarets and Ritter Range country would have been opened up if Forest Highway 100 had been built.

Back Country Manners

"When I ride out of the mountains,
I'll leave only hoof prints, take only memories."

This is the Horseman's Creed used in the University of Wyoming's Packing and Outfitting Field Manual, and it about says it all.

The joy and strength of the wilderness is the feeling that you are the first person to see this wonderful land, but in order to keep it that way you have to practice "back country manners."

These include such basics as how to behave on a trail, how and where to set up camp in a manner to protect watersheds and the environment, where to graze livestock, locate a latrine, build campfires, dispose of refuse and other ways to behave in the mountains in order to keep the land the way God made it.

People who know me say that when I leave a place it is just like I never set foot there. They kid me and say I should have been an old lady, but that's the way I am.

In the back country, I try to use a camp that has been established already, if it is in the proper place. We always had favorites places away from the edge of water. Although I have heard of one commercial packer doing it, if someone is there already, you never ride up and say "This is our camp, you're going to have to move." You go around and find another place where you won't bother the other people, some place where you can keep the mules away from their camp and yours.

Today, most people want to camp in a meadow, right next to a stream or a lake. An old camp on the edge of the meadow is out as far as I'm concerned. I take those camps apart and make it look like they were never there. I've obliterated so many fire rings over the years.

"Gosh, Johnny," people say, "why are you doing that? The Park established that camp."

"No," I tell them, "the Park did not. Someone who was too lazy or too dumb made a camp here."

Where they had some rounds for seats and things, I've taken them off and hidden them or taken them to a camp which was started by the rangers in a proper place up in the rocks.

Whenever I see anyone looking for a camp down by a meadow, whether it's a backpacker or a stock user, I encourage him to go back where it's dry and they're not destroying the beauty. Camping so close to water pollutes, crushes the flowers and destroys the mountain meadows. Regulations in both the Park and the Forest say camps must be at least 100 feet from streams, lakes or trails. That's still too close. Rules and common sense say you should protect the meadows and the only way you can do that is to not camp in them.

The Indians, sheepherders and cattlemen who grazed their stock in what now is Yosemite and the mountain men who grew up with the Park camped further away in open, dry places on a sand flat where the ground is hard and not soft and mushy, like it is near a meadow. You can tell because that's where you find obsidian and other Indian signs. I've been told that by Indians I've known over the years and I've seen it myself. They took care of the land when they camped.

Indians knew a lot more about living in the mountains than some of us give them credit for. They were the first earthmen. They knew the meaning of things. We should listen to them.

Sure, when you camp back away from streams and lakes, you have to carry water, but places like that are warmer, less moist, and have a lot fewer

Packer Bob Barrett leads a string away from the trail to a campsite out of sight in the rocks.

Jim Snyder's survey crew establishes a camp back from the trail and water where it will cause no damage.

mosquitoes which make both people and horses more comfortable. Camping next to water is ridiculous. If you have to walk 100 yards or more to water, that's fine with me. I've had camps with water a couple of hundred yards away. You don't use that much water in a camp. I've had guys come up when I set up camp like that and say, "Okay, Johnny, you carry the water." I tell them that I will, if they're too lazy.

If I am where there is no established camp, I look for a place in the trees or among the rocks, kind of up above and back away from the meadow. I get a feeling about a place as I ride into it. It's hard to explain, but it feels right, combining what you think your party would like with what you feel. Think about what camping on that spot will do to the environment. Are there any little dry washes or drainages? I may be finicky, but I don't want to camp in a place where there are even signs of a dried up little tributary to a creek. And, don't put your horses in such a place, either. Come winter and snow, there will be runoff for two or three months and the pollution will wash down into the main stream.

Look for a place where there is a little breeze going to blow at you. That keeps things cool and nice. But, make sure they can lay out sleeping bags so the breeze doesn't blow down their necks all night. I like a spot where you can look across to a nice view, but far enough away from the trail to be out of sight. Your camp should not spoil the view for others who may be riding through. There may be rocks around, but in between, there are large level areas which are clear and clean and good for setting up a camp. Being in among the rocks, there's no dust around. It's nice and clean.

Whatever you do, stop early enough in the day so your party will have time to enjoy the site.

As you set up camp, find a clump of bushes or rocks where the ground is soft enough to dig a latrine. If you are not staying for a long time, it doesn't have to be a deep pit, but make sure everyone who goes takes a shovel to dig a good sized hole six inches or deeper and to cover it up well with dirt or rock. There's nothing worse than coming into a camp site where there's toilet paper all over the place. It must be at least a good distance from camp — the Park Service manual says 100 feet from water sources, camp or trails. It should be more. The walk will do you good. Again, there must be no sign of any dry drainage where it will get into a waterway.

On the trail, you may not want to unpack a shovel or, if you are on a day hike with your camera, you can't carry a shovel everywhere. So remember what a little kitty cat does around home and dig a hole with a stick or something and then cover it up like the kitty does.

When you wash your face, take your basin away from camp and empty it around a tree in pine needles so it will go into the ground and won't get into any drainage area. Do the same with your dirty dish water. I don't want any soapy stuff near a dry channel. When the snow comes, it would eventually wash on down to the creek. Remember, you shouldn't use any kind of soap, even biodegradable stuff, in streams or lakes.

When you pick your site, unpack. Sometimes I leave the pack mules outside a couple hundred feet or more and carry the gear in. Other times I bring in just one mule at a time. That way you don't have a mess in camp. Bring in the water and roll out the bed rolls and tents, set up your little Coleman stove on a bare rock and settle in.

Camps located in the proper place usually will have a fire ring. Although it is so much easier and cleaner to cook over Coleman stoves, sitting around a campfire in the evening is most enjoyable. Travelers have done it for centuries. There's nothing wrong with that, as long as you don't build a fire near a tree or something that will scorch. But when some guy out there fishing by a creek or a glacier-fed lake picks up some sticks and builds a fire because he's a little cold, he should have gone back to camp. Fires in meadows and along creek banks cause damage.

When you leave, there should be no signs that man or animal has ever been there. Where the ground may have been raked clean of sticks, pine needles and little stones for placing a tent or a sleeping bag, rake them back so the ground looks just like it did when you came into camp. I figure if God dropped those needles there, that's where He meant them to be.

Where the livestock have been tied for packing and unpacking, or they have been picketed or staked, rake out the manure and cover it with dirt and pine needles. Yosemite requires users of livestock in the wilderness to carry both a shovel and a rake. You probably will see a shovel on the load, — I've even seen parties without one — but how many rakes do you see being packed in? Very few.

Before we leave a camp, the packers and I would walk around to make sure everything was picked up, even if it held us up an hour or so. If you kept a camp clean, it won't take long. You know, the little kids would get right into that. Young ones like to help. They are sweethearts.

"That's the law of the land," I'd tell them. "That's back country manners. You wouldn't put this kind of stuff in your playroom at home, would you?"

In addition to the required shovel and rake, a broom comes in handy in camp.
(Photo courtesy of Dr. Barton A. Brown.)

Sometimes the parents would ask, "Why don't the rangers pick up after us?" and I would explain that they have lots of other things to do and it is our responsibility to leave a good camp because some of our good friends might be the next campers to come here. Then the parents would get in and help too. You know, if you set a good image, the others will follow. It always worked.

At one time campers could burn and bury garbage in both the Park and the National Forest. I never believed in that. Old Mr. Bear would come around and dig it up and there it is. One time when I was a kid, I saw a bear who had dug up a syrup can and was sucking the rest of the sweet stuff out of it. I hung around until he was done and went about his business so I could get the can. For a long time, I had it at Beasore hanging up to show people where Old Mr. Bear had put his teeth into it. We carried out all our garbage for years and years, long before it became a requirement.

Two things that drove me crazy were tinfoil around the fire and cigarette butts, especially filters. If I complained to my guys or the party, some would get on me.

"I know you have to smoke," I would say, "but pick up the butts before you leave. We're going to sit here and pick them all up even if it takes till dark, and we are going to take them out in the garbage bags."

If you leave a camp site proper and clean, with the fire ring in the right place, the next people who come along will see how it should be done and learn.

Backpackers generally are pretty nice but need educating too. These rules apply to them as well as to those of us who use stock. A lot of people blame livestock for all the problems on the trail, but I've always loved to hike and when I travel cross country on foot, I find backpackers' little fire rings with tinfoil, maybe a sock, britches or something they didn't pack out. There haven't been horses or mules on the Mt. Whitney trail for more than 25 years, and yet I understand the trail is more like a sewer than anything, filled with trash, human waste, toilet paper and litter.

Back country manners mean that we should pick up anything we find around any camp site or on the trail whether it was ours or someone else's. It's our responsibility to help keep the wilderness clean and nice. Whenever my guys met anyone of the trail, they would tell them, "Take care of our beautiful mountains while you are having a nice time." Sometimes, after telling them the law of the land about cleaning up, I'd tell them:

"You never know, sometimes the rangers hide back in there where you can't see them and watch you with field glasses and if you mess up they'll come in and cite you. They are getting tough on us guides and other people back here

54

in the wilderness."

The next time through there, we would check their camp. Sometimes it worked and they left a good camp, but too often we would have to clean it up. We always carried an extra gunny sack or two for trash and many's the time we've packed out a sack or two of trash left by others.

Every fall, after hunting season, we would make a swing through the back country just to take out other people's trash. I remember one time when I went in with Keith Soward, the Oakland artist who has been a friend since we both were kids at Beasore. We met a ding-a-ling pack string coming out, and I told Keith that the way that outfit looked we would find a mess ahead of us. On that swing, we took home three mule loads of trash, a lot of it from that packer's camp. This was a commercial operator who was supposed to know what he was doing. It is the duty of everyone of us who love the mountains to care for them so there always will be wilderness.

I feel strongly that both the Park and the National Forest should charge for wilderness permits and then put the money right back into educating the people, backpackers and stock users alike, on how to care for our mountains.

I also would use that money to hire a bunch of young kids and put them under someone who knows the mountains and let them spend the summer hauling out trash. There's a lot of bottles, cans, barbed wire and worse trash hidden away back there. We have to clean it up and it's going to cost money. This way people who use the wilderness will help preserve it.

The clean-up crew should be put under a man who really knows the mountains and what he is doing. It's just like putting a man up there to fix trails, he has got to know what he's doing. If he doesn't know anything except to cut a few little limbs off the trail and this and that, it's no good. You need experienced men of top caliber leading and training these crews. Let them school a young guy, letting him do the rough work and learn. Then he becomes the professor for the next generation, a man who knows what he is doing.

I know the Forest Service has a tougher time keeping things cleaned up than the Park does, because they have lots of users other than just those who want to go back and enjoy the high country. They have to deal with hunters, loggers, woodcutters, miners and a lot of other people outside of the wilderness areas. Inside the wilderness and outside people with stock camp back over the hill and the new rangers don't know where to look for them. There is so much abuse.

But, they are too lax. Look at loggers, for instance. Why doesn't the Forest Service make them pick up their messy oil cans and old cable that breaks back.

there and the mess they leave. I've picked up cans along the road and I've seen rangers who could do it, but they just won't. They just zoom right through. Maybe it isn't their job, but gee whiz, it is their country. If they won't do it, they should make the loggers do it. I know loggers work hard trying to make a living, but they've left some of the damnedest messes you've seen in all your life.

I keep coming back to back country manners as important to the enjoyment and the preservation of our wilderness areas and the rest of the mountains, but I believe that those who want to go into the high country have to learn what's right.

If I wanted to go to the city and be a candlestick maker, I'd have to study real hard to learn how things are done, learn the proper guidelines and rules and what kind of behavior is expected of me in the city. It's the same thing up here in the mountains where back country use is exploding. Some say I'm too radical. Maybe I am a little, but I don't think so, because I love the Park and Nature so. It's kind of bred into me. I'm looking to the future. I'm caring about the kids and grandkids and great grandkids. There's not going to be anything left if we don't start educating them.

Even as a young kid, I always wanted the mountains to stay the way they were then. I know there has to be some changes because we have so many people from all walks of life who need the wilderness and an opportunity to get out of the cities. They are discovering that the strength of the mountains and wilderness experience is that the traveler can feel that the land today is the way it was when man first saw the mountains. But, we've got to keep it that way. Protecting the back country basically is common sense and courtesy or, as I call it, "back country manners," which people have to practice if we are to preserve that spirit.

On The Trail & In Camp

The Yosemite Park wilderness brochure about traveling in the back country merely says go single file, stay on the trail, don't take shortcuts; hikers should give way to livestock, standing on the uphill side of the trail; and leave your bikes, motorized or not, at home.

It's all good advice based on solid reasons, but there is so much more people should know about traveling through the wilderness so that they may get the greatest pleasure and benefit out of their experience.

Whether you are traveling with stock or with a backpack, keep your eyes open, look around you. When you love the terrain, watch everything and enjoy it. Mark in your head a certain rock, a snag, a peak, a creek and in that way you make your own mental map, noting special things that will bring back memories of your trip and guide you if you want to travel the same route again. I know there are lots of maps, but if you watch the landscape and use it for markers, it will give you a better feel for the wilderness. I grew up that way. You get so you pick it up real easy just by looking.

You see, there were not many markers on trails years ago and on a lot of trails there were none at all. Old mountain men, sheep-herders, cattlemen and Indians didn't have maps. They didn't need them, they had a sense of geography.

Jim Snyder, who is cataloging blazes and other historic objects in a Yosemite wilderness survey, talks about the fact that in the early days maps were an oral tradition. Mountain men didn't rely on blazes to mark their trails then. They traveled by geographic landmarks they learned by personal experience or word of mouth. Blazes weren't used until the soldiers arrived in Yosemite in the 1890s. The old timers said the

"T" blaze carved in a lodgepole pine by U.S. cavalrymen about 100 years ago.
(Photo by Jim Snyder)

army's "T" blazes were to make sure the soldiers found their way home.

As recent as the late 1920s and early 1930s, when I started packing, trails weren't marked too well. The main trail to Givens Lake, for instance, actually was no trail at all to speak of. A lot of the lakes had been stocked with fish by sheepherders. Later, when they were named by rangers, the names didn't show up on early maps, so you had to rely on your knowledge of the terrain and landmarks.

Staying on the trail single file, whether riding or walking, is important because that way you won't cause additional damage to the countryside. I've seen trails through meadows that have been like six-lane highways. Either the original trail got a little damp so hikers started another or people spread out. Walking side by side may be pleasant, but it sure messes up a meadow.

Groups traveling together with stock should keep together, don't anyone just ride out there in front or let the caboose drag behind. Those leading should look back, keep people up, spaced a couple of horse lengths apart — not too close to their heels; give them a little room. Don't go off and leave one way back there.

Make enough pit stops so no one has to drop behind. Pity the poor guy who has to stop way back. While he's doing his thing, the poor horse is raring and yanking on him wanting to catch up with the rest of his buddies. Stay and stop together. A guide should know the country well enough to find a place that has some easy-to-get-to dense bushes for the ladies and tell the guys to go down behind the rocks. Even people who don't know the country can watch for the right places as they go along.

When passing another string or a group of backpackers on the trail, whoever has the handiest place should get off the trail, if there's room. I know the regulations give livestock the right of way, but sometimes you meet a bunch of kids who don't know anything about the mountains. They always are a little bit afraid of animals, but I've seen back packers walk right up to your horse, refusing to get off the trail. I don't know if they were maybe a little bit leery of getting lost or somebody told them they had to stay on the trail or whatever, but they wouldn't budge. So, if there was any room, we'd always move over. Or, when you meet another pack train, we'd always get out of the way and let them pass without hurting somebody.

Following another party too close is bad. I never did like anybody following me. If we see somebody coming we'd try to speed up or pull off and let them go by. You don't want anybody tailgating you when you're driving. On an old dusty road, you don't want to stay where your dust is just fogging them up. It's the same thing.

Wherever you are, stop and pick up even little scraps of paper. On the trail, stopping works two ways. Not only do you pick up the litter, but you give the horses a little rest and it's good for riders, especially novices, to get off that horse once in a while and walk around a little.

When leading a string of pack animals, some old timers used to, and I believe some packers in the Rocky Mountains still do, tie a mule's lead rope to the tail of the pack animal in front of him. I never liked that because one time early in the game, I was checking out a mule and his tail was pulled out. The joint was loose and he didn't have any control over his tail. There are better ways of doing it. Some people like to tie the lead rope to a yoke up on the neck of the animal ahead. I don't because when one pulls back, the shoulders get sore.

The way I like is to braid a pigtail out of light, soft rope. It even can be baling twine. Hook this to the lead hickey on the back of the pack saddle and tie the lead rope of the following mule to it. If a mule gets in trouble or falls, the pigtail will break and he doesn't pull the whole string over.

When the going gets tough, switchbacks are bad, the rock work is about ready to go, leading a string through, tied together, can get dangerous. A rock

A multi-lane "highway" through a meadow is one of the abuses found in the wilderness.					*(Photo by Jim Snyder)*

moves under a mule's foot on a bad switchback and he will hold back. The packer doesn't give him time and the mules get pulled over the top. Ridiculous. Those boulders start to move and you could roll them right over the people and stock down below hurting or killing them.

I saw that happen at Red Peak Pass. Some kid was all dressed up in a hat and boots and thought he was a packer. He didn't know what he was doing and tried to lead a string through all hooked up. He had a big wreck. He killed a mule, pulling him over the switchback. I've seen some bad wrecks around Junction Buttes, near Sheep Crossing, over in the Ritter Range country and all around. So many times, people will just leave the dead mule by the trail to stink up the whole Park. My guys have pulled many dead mules off the trail, into the brush and notified the rangers to come and put slack lime on them.

An experienced guide should know the terrain ahead. If he knows what he is doing, he will cut the string loose before he gets into a mess. This way each mule can feel his way. In that type of country you must have all your mules kind and gentle. If not, you have to lead them through one at a time.

When loose herding or leading them through a tough place like that, I muzzle them so they won't fool around getting grass. The muzzle is snapped to the bridle out of the way until you need it and all you do is pull it over and snap it in place. It keeps them moving.

You, or anyone else should be able to walk up to your mules and catch them on the other side of a bad spot, or any other place, for that matter. I won't have a mule that is hard to catch. A bad-mannered horse or mule should not even be in the mountains.

Another problem with inexperienced horsemen, such as the flatlanders who buy an animal at a saleyard and head right for the mountains, is azoturia or "kitty lock." We've come across people, hunters primarily, who are pushing their animals too hard. "Hey, that horse is all sweaty," I'll tell them and talk to them real nice about what to do for it.

"Oh, we bought this thing and we got to get in to get our buck," they say.

We get our party spotted in and come back through and the horse is dead. You can tell how good a horseman or a mountain man is by how he takes care of his animals. If he doesn't take care of his stóck, he won't take care of the mountains.

Flatlander stock feel the altitude just as much as humans do. A lot of times when you go from the Valley to the high country, you feel it for a day or two. Horses and mules do too. Also remember that when you get up there you eat like a bear. Horses and mules use a lot of energy in the mountains too. You've got to provide good food for your stock. That's why I always carry grain — it also helps to catch in the morning — and turn the animals loose up in the rocks where there is a lot of bunch grass. Bunch grass has little seeds and a lot of food value. They may have to work a little harder for it, but there are places where it's thick and they fill up quicker than they do in meadows. Stock don't do well in meadows because the water content in meadow grass is so high and the food value is so low. It is just wishy-washy. If given a choice, mountain-smart livestock will move up in the canyons.

I notice that even down in the lower elevations where they may be on private meadow land that's wet, they don't do well at all. I learned that from the old timers, but later when I packed veterinary professors from Davis and CalPoly, they confirmed that.

Anyhow, I don't like to see the stock in the wildflowers.

A major problem develops when private stock users or commercial packers go off and leave some of their animals alone in camp. You cannot do that. Somebody should stay around the camp and horses at all times. If you want to go fishing, take turns. When some of the horses go, the ones left get scared of being abandoned. If tied to a picket line, stake or tree, those left behind are just going to rare and dig and jump around and dig holes. They paw, paw, paw and get roots bleeding. And, if they are not tied right, they are going to get tangled up and fall and hurt themselves. I once saw a horse that had been tied like that near a creek. It got tangled up, fell in and drowned.

Some people solve this problem by picketing by a front ankle to a stake, small tree or some such thing so the line remains low. But, the animal must be broke to this type of picketing or he will chafe and hurt his leg.

If you have to picket an animal, tie a lash line or two as high as you can reach between two trees small enough so that you can bend them toward each other and keep the tension on the picket line. Put a bowline in the lead rope so the horse can move back and forth the full length of the line. Picket only one horse at a time that way. This way he has fifty or more feet to move about and graze. The trees should have enough spring in them that he can lower his head to feed, but keep the lead rope off the ground when he raises his head. This way he never gets tangled up.

A lot of times, if I have to tie to a single tree, I use one in the middle of some slick rock so the horse will not damage anything he paws.

If they had barriers or smooth wire drift fences like they used to have in the Park, stock could be turned loose. Some of these were just gates across narrow spots in the trail, mostly made with natural things, like little lodge poles, while others used smooth wire. Charlie Gilmore was quite a hand who worked for both the Curry Company and the Park Service. He was noted for gates he made in the mid 1950s out of poles from around the trail with branch forks for hinges. They fit right into the environment.

Other barriers got the stock away from the trails and gave them room enough so that they didn't congregate in any one area. As a result, I never saw any signs of abuse to the land. Where stock was held away from the trail you couldn't hardly find any tracks. They would be up on a slope a half a mile or more from the stream. It's the nature of horses used to the mountains to go up a draw and get away from the mosquitoes. There is no telling where a horse that is not used to the mountains will go.

If you turn your stock loose a half a mile or a mile away from camp, you probably wouldn't see them, but could hear your bell horse or mule a mile or two up the canyon. And, make sure they are up above your camp. Always listen to the bells. If you hear them ringing faster, you know they have their bellies full and they may be headed for home. If they are above camp, you can run out and head them off before they get to the trail. Otherwise, you may have a long walk. Usually, you should have a horse that you can trust to stick around and the rest will stay with him.

Some guys insist on having the stock in sight all the time and will stick them right on the main trail where they can see them from camp. It's ridiculous. If stock has been pastured together throughout the winter, they usually stay around anyway. If you want, you can hobble one or two leaders and the rest will stay with them, but remember, with regular hobbles they can travel pretty fast and far.

I like the Apache hobble over the back or a drag hobble. They slow them down. The Apache is best. You put a loop around one forearm and cross another loop around the other forearm and lead the ends over the horse's back, tying it rather tight on the back. This way he can move and graze comfortably, but if he takes too large a step, he will feel it on his back. If your horse is still too active, you can tie more knots, four, five, six square knots, over the back. That'll slow him down. A drag hobble is just a piece of chain, maybe three feet long, hooked to a front leg. If the animal moves too fast, he steps on it.

What it come down to is I don't really like hobbles or picketing. The best thing to do is to turn them loose. If you treat them right, they won't go home on you. You may have to walk a little to bring them in, but in the morning I always know where to find them. Look up where the sun first hits the side of the canyon. That's where they'll be, eating a little of the bunch grass, and getting warm in the morning sun.

One more thing about handling stock in the back country. They are going to have to have water, but I don't like to see livestock going out into a lake and

Packer Bob Barrett repairs a Charlie Gilmore gate made all of natural materials.

it upsets me when I see someone driving a whole bunch of stock into a stream. I've seen people and I've seen horses go into lakes and I just make them get out of there. I may be funny about that, but I want nothing from the horse going into that lake or stream. There are tributaries where you can lead them to a standing pool and water the stock without stirring things up too much. But always water your stock down stream from where you were getting your camp water. On a few occasions, I've even carried water to stock in a five-gallon can.

I know that the bear and the deer go, and you can't stop them from doing it when they've got to go, but I can keep the horses out of the water.

"Johnny," some of the guys say, "you're just too finicky. How many times have you drank water on the ranch where there is an old dead cow up there."

"Maybe I've done that on the ranch. You never know," I say, "but this is different. You've got the public. This Park or this National Forest belongs to the people, all of us. We've got to take care of it. I know I get carried away. I am a little funny, but that's just the way it is."

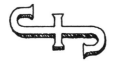

Apache hobble keeps stock from moving too far or too fast.

My brother Joe and I at Bass Lake.

Tricks of the Trade

From when I was a little kid, I learned from old timers. Most of them were Indian or part-Indian and knew about the mountains. North Fork Indians like Pinky Bethel and Otis Teaford were super guys and knew so much.

Those old guys were so funny. I've seen mechanics who if they don't like the smart-aleck kid that comes along they aren't going to tell him anything. Those old packers and the Indians were the same way. They wouldn't tell you anything until they got to know you. If they didn't like a kid, they wouldn't even let him play with their kids. Tom Jones was half Indian so they kind of accepted me, but still I had to be real nice when I asked them something.

"Mr. so-in-so," I would say, "why do you do this or how do you do that?"

They got so when I asked them they would tell me and then come up with something else that would help me more. They taught me so much about so many things. Some were just little day-to-day things that I came to do naturally, like reading the landscape. Others were special things, like how to track people or prevent people from tracking you.

If you are going to a special place to enjoy the mountains or to camp or fish, for instance, you don't want to leave any tracks regardless of whether you are riding or walking. A lot of people think they can fool someone if they turn off the trail on slick rock or in a creek, but Indians taught me not to just do that. Be a Wiley Coyote and send some people up the trail to make some other tracks and confuse them.

In one of his reports on the Yosemite Park Wilderness Historic Resources Survey, Historian Jim Snyder quotes Robert Bright, who ran sheep in the Park years ago:

"It was simple to get into the Park, even though the cavalry was looking for us. We simply took the bells off the sheep and brushed the trail behind them." To this Jimmy added, "Was this not similar to the actions of early day packers to hide their prize lakes, fishing spots, etc., not only going over slick rock when they left established trails, but maybe brushing trails behind them?"

He's right, but it still can be pretty hard to hide a favorite lake or stream from an old time mountain man.

I remember a couple of times years ago when I surprised people in their favorite fishing holes. One time I was headed for Ottoway with Fibber McGee and Molly. About half way there, we met two ladies and a man coming down the trail. Later, I found out one was Mary Curry Tresidder, daughter of the founders and a part owner of the Yosemite Park & Curry Company. She was quite a mountain lady who packed in every year well into her 80s, I believe. They pulled off to let us pass. About a mile or so up the trail, I lost their track.

We were going to spend a couple of days at Ottoway and while there I went back down and put the Indian sign on them and tracked them. They had come on to the trail over a big rock. I tracked them across into a meadow and to a nice lake with some big Brook Trout in there. This, I found out, was Mrs. Tresidder's favorite place.

I went back again only one more time in my whole life and found Dr. Chester Moyle of Merced there. I never told anyone about this place. Mrs. Tresidder and old Doc Moyle were nice people. I'd sold Doc a mule or two before. Matter of fact, I first met him when I got bucked off a horse in Merced and he sewed my eye up.

"If you were a punk fighter," Doc had said, "I'd just take one stitch, but you're an old rancher and I'll sew it up pretty good."

Another time, I was touring; going over Donahue Pass for Vogelsang. Up above Washburn Lake I saw some old horse sign in the rocks. I went on, but I marked the place in my head. A few years later I was back up there and told my party we were going to rest awhile. I got off and went back in and found a guy sitting there fishing in the river. The fish were really jumping.

Dr. Jefferson Wells of Merced looked up and said "I'll be damned. I should have known a guy like you would find my camp, but I'm glad it was you, because you'll take care of it."

I did. You should respect other people's favorite places. You can go back a time or two yourself, but don't tell everybody about them. They are too nice to abuse by over use.

When you find a special place, you mark in your head just where it is and how to get there. When I first started going out as a little kid I traveled with old Indians and they would say, "Stop. Hey son, remember that rock. Don't forget that tree, remember that bend in the creek, that little turn in the trail, something different." I would ask Tom Jones or Pinky Bethel or whoever, "What about that rock?"

"Well, when you grow up, you might want to bring somebody back here and that's how you'd find the way," they would explain. As I got older, I caught on pretty fast. You have to register in your head that you turn off at certain landmarks. That's how the Indians have traveled for hundreds of years.

When you are traveling up the trail, you not only should watch the landmarks, but the tracks in the trail to see who came this way last. You can tell what's going on ahead of you. Or, sometimes behind you. You know people say there are no mountain lions up there, and I've only seen two in my whole life and one of them was in the road down near Raymond. Traveling the trail once in a while you used to see signs of kills where they had taken what they wanted around the lungs, cut them up a little bit and come back for a second feed; leave the rest for the coyotes and the buzzards. Now days you go up the trail and when you come back you will see where at least one and sometimes three of them have followed your tracks. They would have been standing in the bushes by the trail watching you go by.

It's important also to look back the way you came. The country looks different when you look back on it. I recall, my nephew, Mike Alberta, went out with a ranger looking for a sick girl who was holed up in a blue tent near the Booth Lake Loop Trail up near Vogelsang. It was snowing pretty good when they made the loop with no sign of her. The ranger wanted to go look some place else, but Mike insisted on going back around the other way. Sure enough, they found her easily. Her little tent was up against a big rock. The snow had drifted in so that going one way you couldn't see it from the trail, unless you looked back. It was plain as day going back.

Indians also taught me when you are searching for someone who is missing or injured you work in a circle, especially if you are alone. First, you have to pick an area based on what you know about the person, where they were last seen and the terrain. Then hike in a circle, starting about a mile out from the center. Slowly work round and round, closing in until you get to the hub. Every once in a while, stop and listen. Listen hard. You can do that best when you are on foot. When looking for people, if there is a little breeze they may be crying or hollering. I've found several people lost or injured that way.

I recall a girl with compound fractures and a bad cut on her head. She had fallen off a cliff and had been out there for two and a half days. She and her boyfriend were out hiking when she fell and he left her to come in for help. It took him part of a day and all the next night to get to Beasore. He was so messed up he couldn't tell us exactly where she was. Early in the morning the rangers came and we went off with the kid. I thought about how he described the country and remembered a couple of days earlier where I had seen evidence of a camp. When we got up there, I began to make a big loop on foot the way the Indians had taught me. After a while, I heard a little whimper and knew I found her, but I didn't want to go right up to her and shock her, so I made a noise like a bird or something, until she said "Who's there?"

I told her everything was all right and we were going to get her out just fine. I had to leave her to go find the rangers. They were traveling in a pack, headed in the wrong direction. We went back and got a basket stretcher, got her into it all covered up with blankets, and put her on top of my horse. It was all downhill to the road, so I put her head over the rump so she would rest easier. We strapped her down real tight so that the fractures wouldn't get worse. By that time, the sun had gone down, so I led the horse out in the dark. Part way down, I saw a light ahead and Denny Peckinpah was coming up the trail with a Coleman lantern. He had heard we were bringing her out and came to help.

We got her out to the ambulance and she got well, but it was rough. I thank God for the helicopter ambulances today.

You look for a horse the same way, except you can ride and cover ground much faster. Horses are funny, especially those valley horses. If they are from a pack station or a Yosemite Park horse, they know the way home, but when private stock gets loose there is no telling where those dummies will go. Sometimes you can track them.

One time, some guys from Hollywood, including horse trainer Clyde Kennedy, had been camping in the back country. When it came time to leave, they were missing three horses. For a while they came up on weekends and couldn't find them. Late in November, I went looking. I was lucky, I was able to track them, even though the tracks were three months old. They had gone over kind of a cliff down into the Merced River Canyon. They went down for water and didn't have enough brains to go back out the same way. Lucky there was water and a little meadow there, but even so they were nearly starved to death. I had a tough time leading them back up out over the cliff, but they came. Their owners could hardly believe it. When you are rounding up the last of the range cattle who are scattered, you work in the same way, in a big circle.

One more thing, you have to learn to read your horses and mules and the old timers showed me that the only way you can do that is to sit out there and watch them, just like a sheepherder. A lot of people don't know how to read their animals and that gets them in trouble. For instance, if you get an agitator who starts to head for home when he gets his stomach full, get rid of him. Your livestock has got to get along as one big family. If they don't, get some that do and run them together in the winter as well as the summer.

The animals have to have good dispositions. That's No. 1. They have to be 100 percent gentle, even if lightning hits nearby. You don't want any of them that are shell shocked. You find that by reading the stock and the only way you can do this is sitting out there watching them.

Of all the lessons I learned from the Indians, probably the most basic is: "Before you make a move, don't use your legs or your feet, use your brain."

The Long Ears

People used to say that I wasn't interested in anything that didn't have two long ears and a tail.

That's not quite true. I do like horses, but I must say that mules get under your skin. A good mule is a friend, a good faithful friend.

Their ancestors go back to biblical times and work mules helped to build our nation. They say that George Washington, who was first in a lot of things in this country, was the first to breed American mules. He used jacks given to

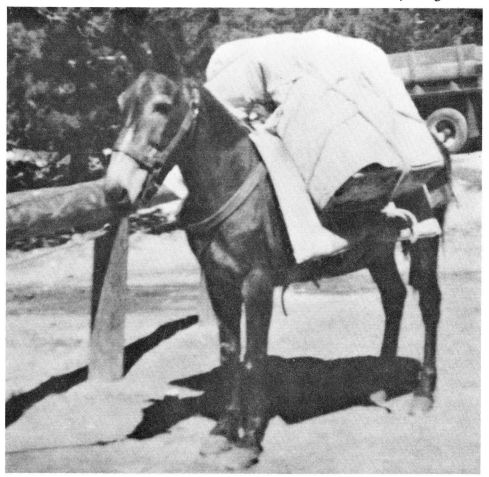

Thirty five years old and still working. A Jones-bred mule carrying linens to Yosemite High Sierra camps.

him by the King of Spain.

Thousands of acres were plowed by mules to make farm fields that fed pioneer families who settled our land. Explorers, trappers and adventurers who moved westward just to see what was on the other side of the mountain were accompanied by mules.

Years ago, there were just the work mules, the plowers and the packers. As the nation grew there came the cart mule, the sugar mule, the cotton mule, the tobacco mule, the logging mule and the mining mule. I read a lot about that one, the little mining mule. When he was young they lowered him down the mine in a net and he would be there all his life; go blind because of the darkness. Yet, like all other mules they would work their hearts out, if you treated them right.

Work, work, work. A mule can wear a horse out so fast. In his life span, a mule will wear out three or four horses. A mule I sold to the Curry Company back when Jess Rust was in charge of the stables was still working at 35 years old, hauling linens in to the High Sierra Camps.

Another pair, Katie and Belle, I shipped out of Amity, Arkansas years ago. When I saw them, they were pulling logs in the mud of those bayous. They were the smallest team they had, a nice, coal black team. They were young then, three and four years old. They would go right down on their bellies and get up and pull, pull, pull. Man, I watched them a couple of days. They didn't want to sell them, but I kept offering more money until I finally got them and brought them on home. I packed with them awhile and then Walt Castle bought them for the Park. Over at Bishop they pulled so hard they broke the double tree.

Jim Snyder with his trail crews pulled a lot of rock with Katie. That Jimmy sure knew how to build trails. Talk about smart, affectionate mules, whenever Katie would see Snyder, she would nuzzle around his pockets until she found an apple. Snyder really loved that mule.

"You know, Katie told me real quick that I was just kind of holding the leather," Jimmy once told me. "Boy, if I did something wrong, she'd turn around and give me the dirtiest damn look you ever saw. I learned a lot from her. I learned what you did do and what you didn't do. She was good."

Katie's still alive. Bob Barrett got her and put her out to pasture. Bob explained, "She'd paid her dues. She deserved a good old age."

Mules are a little hardier, a little tougher than horses because they have that half jackass in them. They are better keepers, don't eat so much. It doesn't make any difference if it's a mule or a hinny, it's still half jackass. The hinny's momma is a jackass. It's daddy is a horse. Some people say a hinny is a little

Jim Snyder hauls rock with his favorite mule, Katie, (top). At Bishop, Katie and Belle pull away with top honors. (Jim Snyder Collection)

better, but they're not. I've raised hinnys. They are easier to breed although sometimes a stallion won't serve a jenny; wants nothing to do with her. So you have to play tricks on him, have a mare in heat along side of him and pull him off and put him on a jenny. A jack some times is the same way with a mare. He runs with the jennies. His species come first. Either way they are so smart. It is the jackass in them. In race horses, the mare may be 65 percent important, but in mules it's 50-50.

Mules are much more sure-footed on the trail and won't get you into trouble or hurt you or themselves. If you overload them they will just lay down on you. You can push a horse across dangerous ground, but you have a time getting a mule to go where he shouldn't. They sense everything, a fracture, a bad place, a cave in. They just won't go. They'll vapor lock on you.

I started working with mules when I was only 5 or 6 driving a hay rake on the West Side of the San Joaquin Valley. I also remember those big old mules my neighbor had to pull grain wagons and the old threshers, with 20 to 24 head on a team.

When I was 16 I bought my first jack. Oh, I had been working with horses and mules all along at Tom Jones' in Beasore, but this was the first that was my own. I've had a lot of jacks and bred a lot of mules since then. Once you are around them, they'll get to you. I don't know what there is about them, but they've got you.

I remember mule teams like this pulling big harvesters.

(McHenry Museum Photo)

74

Originally, mules were all draft animals, but go to Bishop Mule Days today or read Betsy Hutchins' American Donkey and Mule Society magazine, "The Brayer," and you will see all sorts of types — racing mules, jumping mules, performance mules, miniature and mammoth mules, standard size and miniature cart mules and riding mules including those ridden side saddle.

Of course, my favorites are the old standbys, pack mules, even the small ones I kid my friends about. "Lunch mules" I call them. "About all they can carry is your lunch," I tell them. These smaller recreational mules do look a little better than the big old mules. They are classy looking, light on their feet, more fluid, do a good job and are easier to load, especially for a little guy like me, but I do like them a little bigger for packing.

It was the pack string from Yosemite National Park that in the early years really put Bishop Mule Days on the map. Walt Castle set the standard. The Park mules had class, good stock, nice tack, nice clean-cut rangers. When they came down the parade line in those first years, the crowd went wild. They always packed something special. One year they had the Liberty Bell, a bell so big it almost dragged on the ground. Another time it was a great big barrel and another a privy on a "crapper packer." Other packers began to follow, one with a clothes line with all the laundry including lingerie hanging out, another mule carried a bathtub with someone in it. You talk about the cameras flying — zoop, zoop, zoop.

Then every year Walt upgraded and they got better and better. When they got to the packing contest, nobody ever did catch up with that Park bunch. In addition to Mule Days, I judged several state fairs and Los Angeles County, adding up to probably 70 or more events, but I never saw a string that could touch those Yosemite mules Walt Castle had.

For a long time, Bishop didn't give Walt Castle the credit he deserved. I got pretty upset with them over there. Matter of fact, when they named me "Most Honored Packer" in 1985, I tried to turn it down because Walt deserved it more. They sent a couple of kids down to where I was judging and tricked me into the parade. I'm glad they finally did honor Walt in 1991, the spring after he retired at Yosemite.

While judging there, I remember one lady complained to me about not being able to compete against the government mules. I gave her both barrels:

"I been out since I was a little kid and I've seen things like your string, baling wire, canvas cinches, canvas britches and breast collars that tear up a horse or a mule. I figured when I grew up, if I couldn't buy all I wanted, I would get one good saddle that would last me 40 years and one good mule that would last me 20. If that didn't pay I'd go out of business."

Bishop Mule Days parade featured novelty packs such as the Liberty Bell, left, and the Crapper Packer, below. Both were Yosemite Park entries.

(Jim Snyder Collection)

Bishop's Most Honored Packer.

She came back the next year with five new mules, five new saddles, copied Walt's, and got in and started winning.

Mule Days started when the Eastern High Sierra Packers Association decided to find out whose mules were best. A small group of us got together in 1969 to plan the first Bishop Mule Days for the following year. In 1970, we had about 65 mules, now there are 10 times that number. It became a big community event. At first there was competition in packing, cow working, fence mending and driving. Hauling and most performance events seen at western horse shows were added. The finest mules from all over the country were being exhibited, so buying and selling were added. Still later mule racing was included.

Today the program includes working pack trains, packing competition for men and women, saddle mules, steer stopping, box and diamond hitch contests, packing scramble, driving exhibitions, reined mules, musical tires, relay and straight races, model pack and saddle mules, barrel racing, mule shoeing. There are 136 different categories in competition and the parade has 58 different classifications. It's quite an event. As a result of Mule Days, a lot of people have had the opportunity to learn more about mules, what they can do, how to care for them, how to train them.

The key to training and working with a good mule is using the soft touch. A mule never forgets. Paul and Betsy Hutchins' book "The Modern Mule," published by Paul and Betsy's Hee Haw Book Service in Denton, Texas, sums it up perfectly:

"As any mule owner knows, mules are extremely intelligent equines. Sometimes this intelligence is abused. As the mule is smart, he can think of many different ways to get even with the humans that he thinks hate him. However, the same mule, broken firmly and gently will make a willing and affectionate companion for life to humans that treat him properly."

Kindness goes a long way, not only in training, but throughout the rest of their lives. Talk to them low, don't talk loud. I have seen guys holler at mules. It doesn't work. Talk to them low and scratch them as you walk around them. Never strike a young mule, or for that matter you should never strike any mule. If you are going to whip him, never do it from behind because that way you get him to kicking. Just remember that if you treat your mules right they will be your best friends and will stand by you just like your best dog. A mule is something else, the way they'll produce for you.

Pasture your mules and horses together in the winter and every once in a while go out in the field and whistle for them to come to you. Give them a little grain when they do. If you do this at the same time every morning, winter and summer, it will put an alarm clock in there stomachs and they will come looking for grain. Make them come to you. If you can't catch them with a nose bag, I just don't want them. I don't care how nice they are. Actually, I prefer one I can catch without a nose bag, just walk out to him.

When I insist on this, people ask me, "What's your problem, Johnny?"

"Hey, I don't want a problem," I tell them. "When my people want to move, I want to be ready, brushed, saddled and ready to go. I don't want to be out there chasing some mule all over the woods and have people waiting. It's their trip."

Any one that doesn't come to you, get rid of him. No matter if he's the best you've got. Sell him to somebody you know for a ranch horse where they've got corrals.

If they get along as one big family, you won't have any problems when you get in the back country. They'll stay around and won't go home on you. That's the way the old timers did, the old rangers.

Years ago, I had a mule, a red mule. When I went in the back country, I would watch him. The stock would go out and graze and would scatter out nice in the bunch grass and the rocks and wouldn't cause any abuse. They would stay right there. You would think there was a corral there, maybe 50 acres. You couldn't even tell where they had walked in the rocks and hard soil. This red mule, once in a while would call them and come down to camp, bringing them all with him. I would reward them for it. The animals got so when we would stay two or three days in the same place, they would kind of know it's going to be home for that night or two.

In picking a pack or riding mule, the most important thing to look for is personality. That's the same as in people. Also like people, personality shows in their eyes. He has to be an honest, good minded, really docile mule. You can tell an honest mule by the way he works his ears and his eyes. They work together.

When you live with mules, you get so you can read them. Like with people, you have to have a mule that will give of himself. Some are bred lazy and with no heart. That's tough to pick. But, you can if you are around him a while. That's why I never bought a mule the first time I saw him.

I like a mule that's kind and friendly. Some mules are a little spooky. They may make a good mule for a young man, a young packer, but for me I want one that will be easy to catch.

During the off season months, and after I retired in the 1960s, I got to buying mules for the Park, the Curry Company, several National Forests and others. I traveled all through Kansas, Missouri and Arkansas and that country. Working all my life with mules and horses and being so finicky about having something nice that wouldn't hurt a woman or child helped in picking out mules for them.

Guiding veterinary professors from the University of California, Davis, and later Cal Poly taught me about soundness and health of livestock. They invited me to their student clinics where I'd learn about limbs, feet, stifle and things like that and good manners. Long before I packed those professors, I learned from Doctor White, the state veterinarian in Madera. He was from Kansas and knew so much. A real nice fellow. I found out from Doc White and the university professors how much I didn't know about a mule; how dumb I was. But, remember the greatest saying in the world is, "You're never too old to learn."

When I was a kid, I learned the hard way. The first couple of mules I got, I bought from a sales yard and one was a pig crawler. I never bought another mule or a horse at a sales yard. Never sold one there either. Always bought them from the breeder or from the farm.

I never had a mule come back. When I went back East, I would hire a guy on commission who knew the farmers well and would take me around. The first day I would take a saddle horse, walk out and watch the mules. They would run and bray. That would be okay, but if they got up on their hind legs and wanted to jump a little bit I didn't care how good he was I didn't want him.

First, we would ride the mule and then see how he pulled in harness. A lot of them pulled pulpwood. If they pulled in harness, they would pack. Then, I would check their eyes. They might have two good ends and a middle, but between the ears they were mean, mean mules. Like they say, "They could kick your teeth out without hurting your mouth." That meanness will show in their eyes. They have to have a nice toned eye. You want no hawk eyes or sunk-in eyes. Make sure you look closely at his eyes, the Cal Poly and U. C. Davis professors told me. Check the eyes for drugs. A mean mule can be slowed down by drugs or if he is bred lazy, they can hop him up. The vets also taught me to check for arthritis; punch them and move them.

"What are you doing, John," guys would say. "Is that some secret trick you know."

I learned from experience if they pop and creak, you got a problem.

Then I would check their feet, their conformation. A mule, to be good, needs well-sprung ribs, deep flank, lots of heart and lung capacity and a nice fork in front. He has to have good bone. You have to watch that he has a nice set of legs that line up right with no weakness in the knees; see that he has nice square feet. The front feet can't be pigeon-toed or splay footed and in back not too sickle on the hock. That can be hereditary in the jack stock, male or female, because they are so inbred.

You look for type. A pack mule, of course, has got to be strong. Some people like a smaller mule because he is easier to pack, but whether he is 14, 15, or 16 hands high he has to be muscular with good bone and good feet. He has to have a good top line, back and wethers. With a straight back and no wethers, the saddle will ride up on his neck, going down hill. The wethers shouldn't be too beefy, though.

They will tell you at the universities to look for a sloping shoulder so they will have a good stride. When you get those big thick, straight shoulders, they are made for a pulling collar. When a pack or riding mule travels, he has to have some stretch, long strides, good action, fluid like an athlete. It's common sense he should move like an athlete. You don't want a heavy footed mule, or a

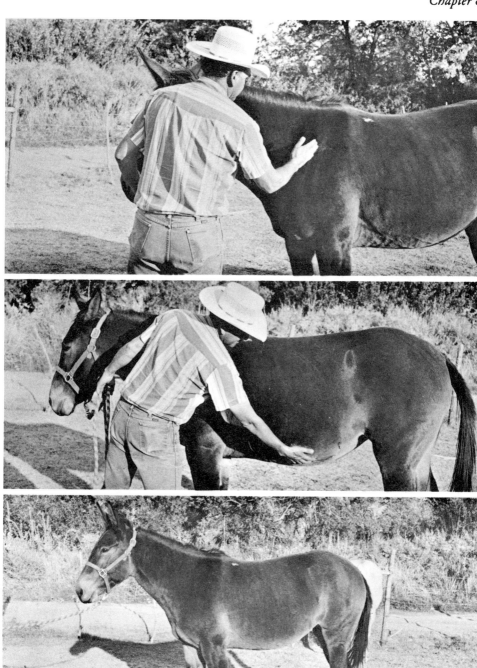

Wayne Tex shows a good sloping shoulder, (top), and good strong side, (middle), and a good back line, (bottom), important points in picking a good mule. The model is Jones-bred.

horse for that matter. I want one that is fluid, fluid, fluid; his feet come off the ground, lots of knee and hock action, like a person who is an athlete.

When I saw some I liked, I'd always come back when the farmer didn't expect me so I could read them before I bought. Sometimes, I would come back several times. That way I could see if they had any problems. As I drove up, I would see them run over and close the barn doors so I couldn't see the bad mules. They were trying to slip something over on me, but they got to admitting, "That little old prune picker from California wasn't so dumb."

"I don't want any pig-crawling mules or jumpers," I'd tell those guys. "You guys are going to be in trouble if I get any."

Pig crawlers are the worst. Sometimes a mule gets crazy about a certain one of his horse buddies. It could be a gelding. It doesn't have to be a mare. Some of them get real jealous and drive other mules away and if you separate him from his buddy, ho, ho, you've got a problem. He'll find a little place that's loose in the fence, a low wire or gap and get down on his knees and crawl under, uprooting the whole fence. They don't care if the barb wire cuts them on the back. A jumper will just go over a fence, that's not so bad, but you still don't want him.

If they have it between the ears, good mules can be trained to pack and to ride. Any mule can be trained to do one or the other, but to be two mules, he has to be real sharp with lots of smarts. Just as important he has to be gentle. I recall in 1956 going back to Phoenix for a big mule sale, taking young Wayne Tex, who was about 15 or 16 years old then. There were some 150 mules or so in the lot. When we got there I told the boy:

"There's some of these mules that will just come up to you, they are so gentle. That's the kind we want, so just don't pay any attention to them, walk away. I don't want these people to think we are favoring anything one way or the other."

Most of these were tobacco mules bought in Tennessee. Farmers would go out and plow with them all day. In the evening when they were ready to go home, they would unhitch the plow or whatever they were using, leave the equipment out there in the field, jump on bareback and trot on home. So, they were all broke to ride. They were some of the best mules we bought during the 1950s. They were good to pack, good to ride, good to shoe, good for any tourist.

A lot of it is in the breeding. If you get one of those really hot mules, bred for riding, he won't make a pack mule because he's too hot. He has too much thoroughbred. He'll run right over you and hurt or kill somebody. If you get one that's half Arab, they're bred too hot too. So you have to have some of the draft breeds in a good pack mule. Remember also, some jack stock, especially that out in the West, has been running wild for years. There's lots of inbreeding and you got to be careful of that. Those can be scary.

Mules are smart. I recall back when Arch Westfall and Vernon "Mogue" Morris were top packers for the Curry Company. In those days, Curry packers drove all their mules. They had a lead mule with a bell. The packer came on behind.

"How can you do that." I asked them. "We just trained them that way," they said. "If the lead mule got to two trails he would stop and shake his tail and wait there until we talked to him. He'd just freeze. We'd say something to him and he'd go on. If it wasn't the right trail, we would say something and he would jump on the other one."

I saw it with my own eyes. I couldn't hardly believe it. It was something.

Another thing about mules. They may be cautious on the trail, but they have lots of courage. You hear more and more talk about bears molesting camps. Well I've known mules that when they were around, bears wouldn't come near. That's not true of all of them, but some were that way.

I remember one time I was over at Sawlog Meadow watching some mules. There were quite a few head of stock around. Toward evening I heard a

Becky, the last saddle mule I bred and raised.

stampede, and here out of the oak came a great big old black bear running like crazy. A white mule with his ears hanging back was running wide open, right after him. The rest of the herd was just kind of running behind to see what was going on. That bear was going so fast he never saw the fence and went clang right through it. The mule let him go then and I had to go out and fix the fence.

Snyder told me old Belle, Katie's partner would kick a bear with both hind legs, broadside, and when that happened the bear never came back. Bob Barrett also had bear-kicking mules.

Riding my world champion, Rabbit, in the high country.

Racing Mules

In breeding of mules, the key is the jackass in them. That's what makes them strong, smart and willing. Certainly that's true in the development of racing and performance mules.

I was curious to see if mules could change gears and run with some speed, so I started a breeding program using the finest athletic, registered jacks available. The mares were registered quarter horses or thoroughbreds. The offspring were registered with the American Mule Association.

But, the greatest mule ever, unbeaten in all-around performance competition for five years in a row, Rabbit, resulted from a wild jack crawling under the fence.

There was a cattleman over in Tehachapi who had pastured a bunch of mares he used to work cattle with. All of a sudden, he came up with a mare with a big belly. He wondered what rodeo he went to where some of his friends had a stallion and pulled a trick on him by breeding the mare. He was really mad. He kept complaining and trying to figure out who did that to him. One morning he and a neighbor went out and the mare had this baby with long ears.

"Didn't you hear the jacks braying once in awhile way over on Tehachapi Mountain?" the neighbor asked when he saw that.

They went over the big field and saw where the jackass left some hair, months ago, when that little desert canary got down on his knees and got his back skinned up coming under the fence looking for the mare. The cattleman was so mad he was going to kill the baby, but the neighbor said no and bought it right there.

This young one, Rabbit, looked like she could run, so when she was three or four years old I bought her. I figured she was out of a good mare and her daddy was wild and had to be an athlete. Those wild jacks could travel. A government man over in Bishop, who was working on cutting down the wild burro herds, told me that they had run some with helicopters to tire them so the ropers could catch them. They had clocked a couple of jacks and a jenny doing 40 miles an hour going through sagebrush and rocks. Those things can fly.

My brother, Joe Alberta, trained Rabbit. Could she fly! When we finally took her to Bishop she was the world champion performance mule five years

With Shirley Green, who rode Rabbit to another victory, and my brother, Joe Alberta, who trained Rabbit.

in a row. In a performance mule, you have to do everything. She was in the barrels, the rein class, stake races, keyholes, everything. Then she had to run the 100-yard race against the world.

That Rabbit was an individual. She was built and she had fire and heart too. She was an athlete. After she started to win everything, I would see these guys from Texas around and they didn't know that I had anything to do with Rabbit. I had told Shirley Green from over at Tollhouse, who always rode her, to tell people it was her mule.

"We're going to beat her next year," guys would tell me. "I've got one that will beat her."

They never did. Five straight years, it was like taking candy from a baby. After that I told Shirley, "Let's just quit. Let's retire her. Let's be fair and not be too greedy." So we did.

But, oh man, while she was running. . . .The ladies loved her. Every time she came down the track for the 100 yards against those thoroughbreds the women would jump up and down on the grandstand, swinging and clapping — some guys too. They'd go crazy.

That mule would jump right out and lead them all the way. They would have caught her though, if she had to go a little further. She was little, a speed mule, a sprint mule. One year, a fellow came in with a fast mule. When he started, he whipped Rabbit over the head and hit Shirley too. Rabbit turned a little, but she outran him anyway. The women were out there and jumped on that guy and cussed him out and fought him. Oh, it was funny. That Shirley was a terrific rider.

The first world champion racing mule I bred and owned was Mosco. The name means mosquito in Mexican. He was world champion for three years until he cut a tendon. Two veterinarians worked on him and he got well, but he came up sore and his little half sister, Cajun Queen, beat him. She went on to win 100 races. She was champion of the world for several years, and as far as I'm concerned still is. She always will be the queen. She was another one I had bred, but I sold her to a trainer for $6,000. She was just coming then and her new owner said "Johnny, she ain't going to run like her brother."

I told him she still was a baby, give her time. When he took her to Bishop, she did well enough that a Texas oil man paid $25,000 for her, I think. The next year she came back and beat her brother.

When I first got interested in racing mules, I went over to Everett Bowman's in Wickenburg, Arizona, one of the big men in breeding fast mules. He was a legend. They tell me he was quite a rodeo cowboy and had a thing for mules.

In the badlands over there, they had wild cattle where horses couldn't go and

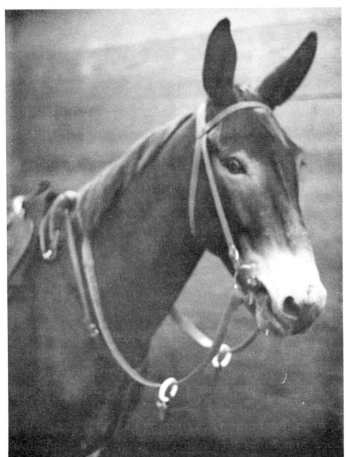

Mosco, a world champion racing mule for three years. Celso Camerena, the jockey, Al Dodd of Sanger and I were partner-owners.

they caught them with these mules. He knew what jack to breed to those good quarter horse mares and thoroughbreds. They would go out in the desert and round up a bunch of stud jacks, look them over for conformation, feet and legs, and try to read them to see how sharp, how talented they were. Then, they would put them in a steer chute in a rodeo arena. They'd open the chute and let him run around a time or two and then open the back gate and the one that could outrun the fastest rodeo ropers was the one they kept for a daddy. That's the one they bred to thoroughbreds, athlete to athlete. It made sense. The one I saw was hidden out in the cactus and the brush. They didn't want anybody to steal that jackass. God, he was a half pint, but talk about fire and wiry.

I first met Mr. Bowman at a Rancho Vista Dores ride years ago when I was there as a wrangler for Huntley and Schwabacher. Rancho Vista Dores was an eye opener. It was big. They were all millionaires. It had everything. They had all kinds of horse shows, quarter horse, thoroughbred and mule races, everything. They got together in groups, rancheros, of maybe 50 or more guys in a separate camp. Each group wanted to beat the other.

Bowman was winning all the match races out in the Arizona buck brush and selling mules to those big shots for $7,000 to $8,000 each. Boy, they got wild when they were betting. It's not pari-mutuel. They were all side bets, this camp against that camp. Stacks of greenbacks, thousands of dollars. I went and took a peek one day. I couldn't believe it and I went out and laid down. After that I stayed out by the horses. I would go ride with them and I'd eat with them, but, oh man, it was nothing for $15,000 to go shuuuuuuush on a bet.

Cajun Queen was a black mule, like her brother Mosco. The year they took her to Rancho Vista Dores, everyone would know her. A rich Nevada casino owner had bought her by then, so he and his jockey took some flour and a little bit of grease and covered her all over so she was a grey.

When it came time to race, they held her back just a little and let the other mules get ahead, but when they turned her loose the flour or powder or whatever just came off in the other mules faces. By the time she hit the finish line a winner she was black again.

A guy was telling me he had looked at that mule and even though she was supposed to be an unknown, he knew something was wrong. He knew she looked like Cajun Queen and at the last minute placed $3,000 on her. He made a killing.

Cajun Queen shows in a futurity race the style that made her unbeaten in more than 100 races.

Recollections

(Editor's note: During the interviews for this book, Johnny Jones insisted on stressing protection of the environment and back country manners. Therefore, these and his experiences with mules make up the bulk of this volume. However, some stories and thoughts unrelated to the basic theme were too good to pass up for they give us an insight to Johnny's way of life.)

INDIAN CAMPS

I always liked to hike. I'd go in the fall when the work was done, and maybe take a pack mule and a friend who liked to fish. He would fish and watch camp all day and I would go; maybe cover 20 miles or more just to see what was on the other side of the mountain. That way I saw and learned a lot about the back country and the Indians. They were all over the Park.

One time three or four of us were right up on top of Triple Divide and we found two great big half spear heads. They didn't match. We left them there. I hope they're still there. I never found out what they were doing there.

Another time, while hiking in the Ritter Ranger right next to the Park I found an Indian camp with obsidian all around. Right near there, I found an old, old log that had been hewed out to make a salt trough. Someone must have slipped into the Park with sheep.

The biggest Indian camp I found was down on the San Joaquin watershed between the North Fork and the Middle Fork, somewhere around Lions Point. I had taken in Dr. Butler and the fighter Young Corbett III. They were fishing, so I took off one day. I crisscrossed everything that day. As it got near dusk, it got to snowing pretty hard. I was about seven miles from camp as the crow flies and headed back cross country.

When I came across this camp, I didn't have time to really look it over, but figured I would come back some day. When I got home, I called an Indian friend of mine, Otis Teaford, and told him about it.

"My God, Johnny," he said, "take me back there. It's my ancestors' camp. They went back and traded for obsidian from over to Mammoth. I heard about it but I never been there. You found it."

"Yeah," I said, "I walked right over the middle of it about dark."

I told Otis how it had pestles still sticking in the rocks, obsidian all over and he said:

"That's the one. The Monos would stay in and hunt and fish all summer and trade acorns for obsidian. They would come down in the fall along the French Trail to the North Fork and into the valley and on to Chowchilla and all around that country. Oh, take me back there."

Otis Teaford was quite a knowledgeable man. It's too bad I didn't get him up there. I got busy and Otis was old then and died before we went back. I never did go back and find it.

The Indians camped a lot at Junction Buttes. I saw a lot of obsidian there. Matter of fact, there used to be an old trail went across there years ago. It went on to Cassidy and across the river on up to Margaret Lakes, all through there and back into the Huntington Lake country.

There were some old blazes back in there. I asked the Forest Service about it but they doubted there was a trail back there. I know it was there. It went by a lake with some big Brook Trout.

FLYING AXES

Some old Indians sure could throw a double bit axe. When I was a kid, Indians were such good axe men. Of course, they only had axes and crosscut saws to cut trees and wood then.

I remember seeing them stick a wood match in a tree and they'd light it throwing an axe maybe 15 feet or so. Jack Frost, an old race car driver from up at Tollhouse, told me he had seen Indians hold a match while another threw an axe and lit it. That was a way of life for them, knives, axes and cross cut saws.

I saw Daniel Jacobs, he was our cook for quite a while, put a little paper pie plate up on a tree about twice the length of this trailer (80 feet or more) and then throw an axe and split that plate right in two. That's

Danny Jacobs

92

when he was 80 years old.

Years ago Danny killed a bear with an axe up at Merced Lake. It was some time in the 1920s. He and a fellow named Sample were back cutting firewood for the ranger camps. Every two weeks or a month, packers were supposed to come in with supplies, but sometimes they didn't. A pesky bear, a big bear, came in and just about cleaned them out. They couldn't shoo him or rock him away.

I know about bears at Merced Lake, 'cause I encountered a bad one that started to chase me a little bit in 1969. They disposed of him later. Anyhow, there was nothing Danny could do to get rid of it and they were running low on food. Danny got along with animals, but this was a cranky old bear who took a swipe at him a time or two as he walked out of camp.

"I may have to kill him with an axe," Danny told his partner.

"No, you'd better not," Sample said. "You better not try because if you wound him he'll kill us."

By golly, a little while later Sample saw Danny filing his old double-bitted axe. Then when the old guy finished it by rubbing the edge on the leather of his high top shoes, whetting it a little bit more, Sample knew what was up.

The next time the old bear came in, the bear hollered and when they moved away, he came at them and stood up. Danny knew that was dangerous and he had to defend himself and wheeeee-u the axe flew. It hit the bear right in the middle of his chest and all you could see was about 18 or 20 inches of axe handle sticking out. The bear started across a log over the Merced River just above the lake, fell in and rolled down into the lake.

All Danny said was: "My axe is at the bottom of the lake."

WOMEN & HORSES

Have you watched the way that women handle a horse? All my life I've noticed that women have a softer touch with horses and mules. Women get along better with them because they are a little on the kinder side. A horse just knows that women are affectionate, which the stock like. A mule is crazy about affection, so they get along great.

I remember I told Bob Barnett when he was with the Curry Company, you'd better hire some women.

"Oh no, you guys, na-na-na-na!" he said, but finally he hired them and they are doing a terrific job. Johanna Wheeler Gehres proved herself as a packer for the Curry Company before becoming the Park's first woman packer. She receives high praise from Bob Barrett in his book on the history of packing in Yosemite National Park.

Women have proved themselves sharp and keen when it comes to handling livestock. I've known some terrific horsewomen. Bishop proves that. There they do so much and outshine the men.

It is because they approach livestock differently than men do. I know men who get a big macho thrill out of controlling a 1,500-pound horse, putting it through its paces. It makes them more manly, I guess. But, you put a woman on that same horse and she will do more with it than the man. When they ride, they will reward and pet them. They will talk to them, scratch them and care for them properly and the horse eats it up and will do most anything for her.

FINDING WINTER STRAYS

(Editor's note: Johnny always pitched in and helped wherever needed. Late in the Fall, after packing season, many was the time he went with a life-long friend, Lester Bissett, to round up Bissett's last stray cattle, often fighting snow and cold before they were through. The opposite page depicts Johnny and Les in a typical scene drawn by Oakland Western Outdoor Artist Evan Keith Soward from accounts Johnny told of these trips, including the following.)

Years ago Les Bissett ran cattle up near Chinquapin, but as old time cattlemen retired he bought their National Forest grazing permits, including O'Neal's and Knox Blasingame's which was 40 miles square, the biggest permit in the Sierra. He had 400 pair there.

Getting them into the high country in the spring was a headache. The Fulmers and others would help him swim the cattle across the Middle Fork of the San Joaquin River. Coming out in the Fall, the river was down which was okay, but if you didn't get them out before it got to snowing you could be in bad shape. I remember one year when we didn't go in for the last strays until December 5. The weather was threatening and by the time we got to Les' upper camp, where we were supposed to stay, there was too much snow. We worked our way down to an old stream guagers cabin near Miller Crossing and the next day got back to McCreary Meadow where Les' dilapidated old truck was. We fought snow all that day in that truck, pulling the horses, using skid

"LAST OF THE WINTER STRAYS"

chains that were all broke up, gunny sacks and even dog chains on the rear duals. Every time we hit a little steep place we'd spin and spin. He'd back up and I'd shovel snow. Finally, we got to Cold Springs Summit about midnight.

"I'm going to ride my horse home" I told Les. "Come on, let's leave this old truck and get out of here"

No, Les wouldn't have anything to do with that idea. He was determined and just as we started down the hill, "BOOM" we hit something. I jumped out to see what's up. The truck's gas tank which sat right in front of the left duals had fallen off. That's what we hit. No lights, pitch dark, I still wanted to go home on my horse, but Les took some baling wire and hung the tank upside down so the damaged part wouldn't leak and drove on home. That's the kind of guy he was. A breed of tough old mountain men you don't find any more.

OUTLAWS

Years ago, I heard the guys talking about an outlaw who was up on the stock drive that used to be the only road into Beasore. His name was Tex. I don't know any more about him other than somebody told me he was white man come in here from Texas. The posse couldn't catch him, so they gave up until somebody told the law to get old Tom Beasore and Tom Jones after him. It was Tom Jones that taught me to track like the Indians and I can track real well, horses, wild animals, people or what.

Anyhow, Tom Jones and Beasore were good. So, they were hired to bring Tex in dead or alive. I don't know whether he had killed somebody or what, but he was a bad one, really a bad one, armed. Jones and Beasore were pretty smart. They tracked him to Tex Meadow — maybe they named the meadow after him, I don't know. Those two were really cagey. They figured it all out where he would hole up, so stayed in the timber and spotted him that evening. He had a horse and a pack. They didn't charge him right away, though, because they knew he was a dead eye and vicious.

They got back in the timber and spent the night. Next morning they hid behind some trees and just waited. The two knew he would come to a little creek for water for coffee or something for breakfast. Sure enough, just about daylight here he comes away from the rocks where he was hiding. Both Tom Jones and Beasore had their guns on him and hollered. He didn't have his gun, just a coffee pot in his hand. He started to run, so they shot him in the leg

Recollections – Photos like these recall many happy hours traveling High Sierra trails.

Loading up for a trip with a group of young people. Traveling with kids always was special for me.

because they didn't want to kill him. They brought him in wounded but alive.

I was told about another outlaw who came into the country and was hard to catch. He was a bad one, a horse thief. The posse tracking him all over never could catch up with him. They got Tom Jones on him. Tom caught up with him, but the outlaw got away again.

You know this horse thief was so smart he put the shoes on his horse backwards. The posse couldn't catch him because they were tracking him the way he had come from, not the way he was going.

YOUNG PEOPLE

Kids always have been special for me. They are our future. When the little ones came around the house, I always talked to them and had something for them, even if it was only a candy bar or a nickel. But, those who worked and cleaned up the landscape were special.

One time going to Fresno, I saw a bunch of kids, a club or Scout group or something, picking up trash along Highway 41. When I came back some hours later, they still were working away. I stopped and talked to their leader and promised the kids they all could come up and ride. They had a great time.

A lot of kids hung around the pack station, picking up, doing odd jobs,

Young Blaine Alberta practices after I've given him a lesson in playing the mouth organ. His dad, Mike, watches.

99

Fishing was good at Horsethief Canyon where Bryan Alberta shows off his catch to me and his father, Mike.

Leading the family pack trip over Red Peak Pass where the kids saw a "bear" with beer can eyes.

some developing into guides and packers. There are several people around who got a start that way. Some have gone into other professions. Those I keep in touch with include a physician in Grass Valley, a lawyer or two, a couple of teachers, several businessmen and, of course, some ranchers and stock people. They all turned out great.

My own nephews started out that way when they still were in grammar school. Every summer I would pick up my brother Joe Alberta's boys, Jeff, Mike, Coleman and David, go into Madera and outfit them with new boots, jeans, shirts and cowboy hats, load them up into the pickup and head for the pack station.

When we got to Bass Lake, the end of the old dirt road up to Beasore and Mugler, the kids jumped out and leap-frogged all the 16 miles up the road picking up the trash. Then they spent most of the rest of the summer in the mountains, riding, working and playing in God's country. It was great for them and I liked having them around.

Once in a while, you could play tricks on them. The best one I remember came during an eight or nine day family pack trip we made late one season. Joe and Gloria, their four boys and daughter, Becky, my wife, Sandy, and my brother Frankie Alberta's son, Francis, went along.

Up at Ottoway, we got caught in a snow storm. We were stuck three days, with only a big tarp spread as a fly for protection. We dragged in a big lightning-struck log and set it afire for heat. The day before we moved on, I snuck out to look at the stock and kept on walking up the trail to the top of Red Peak Pass, a couple of miles with 40 or 50 switchbacks that went up 2,500 feet. I had remembered a sort of cave at the top, and stuck a couple of beer cans in there so the morning light would catch the ends. The next day as we rode up the trail, I talked about bears and had the kids all interested. When we hit the top I said "Hey, look in that cave over there." The little kids thought they had seen a real bear with big eyes looking out at them. I couldn't help laughing so they caught on pretty quick.

A COURAGEOUS DOG

When I was a kid, I spent a lot of evenings sitting around the campfire at Beasore listening to those old buzzards talking about the soldiers and how they treated the sheep men. When the soldiers would catch sheep in the Park, the herders would hide. The soldiers would stampede the animals so the coyotes would scatter and get them.

101

They were talking about a time up near Isberg Pass when the soldiers stampeded a band of sheep. There was a little female sheep dog who would run out and bunch the sheep together again and then the soldiers would scatter them. This happened again and again so the soldiers were going to shoot the dog.

Years ago the old Forest Service rangers got out in the field. This ranger was standing on a peak watching the soldiers. He hollered at them so they knew he was there. When he saw they were going to shoot the dog, he yelled, "Over my dead body. You're not killing that little dog. She's just doing what she's trained for."

Finally they got the sheep over on the National Forest side. In the fall when they came out, this band stopped over at Beasore for a bit and the next day went on to Soquel, about seven miles by trail.

They knew that little female was going to have puppies, but they didn't know when. Going to Soquel, they noticed she was all skinny and gaunt, but she worked the sheep all the way. The next morning she had 11 puppies with her. She had had the puppies up at Beasore and had gone back and forth all night long bringing those puppies down to Soquel — a long, long way to travel.

They hauled her and her puppies home in a buggy. They figured she earned a ride.

Summing Up

I was fortunate to have lived and worked in the high country when it was less populated, life moved at a slower pace and mountain men were a breed of their own. They were true mountain lovers. They were not there working for the money. They did it because they loved the life and gave of themselves to protect the mountains so they could pass them on to future generations.

Today, no other environment offers the unique opportunities to get away from the pressures of our society which is moving at a much too fast a pace. We should do everything possible to keep it that way. People, especially the young in their 30s, 40s and 50s, if they are to survive, need the solitude, the relaxation which only the mountains can give.

But it will take a special kind of person to protect the environment and insure we are not going to destroy our wilderness from overuse and abuse. It's like the old saying I heard one time, "Give me men to match these mountains."

They have to match it in many ways. They have to be like the old mountain people, a man or a woman with a lot of feeling, big inside, sentimental, emotional and with a lot of common sense. Some one who would fight for the wilderness just like a grizzly would fight for his piece of the mountain.

The mountains are God's gift to us. There will be no more like them if we don't preserve them.

Jody Jones favorite photograph of her father.

Johnny Jones, one of last old-time packers, died July 25

Johnny Jones, 74, one of the last old-time High Sierra guides and packers, died Sunday, July 25. Not only did his fame for wilderness knowledge spread throughout the West, he also was an expert in the breeding, raising and training of mules.

Graveside services will be held at 11 a.m. Thursday, July 29, at Oakhill Cemetery.

In the 60-plus years that he traveled the back country trails of Yosemite National Park and the adjoining National Forests, Mr. Jones guided a host of celebrities, including then-Governor and Mrs. Ronald Reagan; radio, film personalities such as Fibber McGee and Molly; authors including Edgar Rice Burroughs; leading professors from the state's veterinary school and many professional people.

The Coarsegold resident was active in the establishment of Bishop's Mule Days and was a frequent judge there. He also judged mules at numerous state fairs throughout the West. In 1985 he was honored as the West's outstanding mule breeder. Among his mules were three world champion racers, Mosco, Cajun Queen and Rabbit. Cajun Queen was champion for five consecutive years and retired unbeaten.

A native of Patterson, Mr. Jones first came to the mountains as a boy of seven or eight when he spent a summer at Beasore Meadows in Eastern Madera County. He never left the hills except to return to school through his first semester of high school. He turned down offers for full time rodeo work and movies because he did not want to leave the area.

Born John Alberta, he adopted the name of his unofficial foster parents, Tom and Ella Jones, with whom he lived and worked for the the next 20 years. They owned the old Jones Store, pack station and campground at Beasore.

In 1953, he went on his own with pack stations in Mugler and Soldier Meadows. Although he sold the stations some 15 or 20 years later, he continued until a year or two ago to guide special groups such as the Reagans, old customers and friends.

In many ways, he was an environmentalist before his time. When he first became a guide in the early 1930's, he insisted upon "back country manners" which, to him, meant protecting the land, grazing stock and camping away from streams and meadows as the Indians did, leaving the landscape without a trace of his visit, and helping others enjoy the beauties of the High Sierra.

"When we break camp, I even rake the pine needles back where they were before we set up," he once said. "If God made those needles fall where they were originally, that's where He meant them to be."

He is survived by one daughter, Jenene Jones of Fresno; two brothers, Frankie Alberta of Oakhurst and Manuel Alberta of Patterson; two sisters, Mary Lindhal of Los Altos and Toni Demoree of San Jose; one grandson and three great grandchildren.

The family requests that any remembrances be made to Fresno Flats Historical Park or the Coarsegold Historical Society.

Sierra Funeral Chapel is in charge of arrangements.

Sierra Star, July 29, 1993